THE FORD COSWORTH

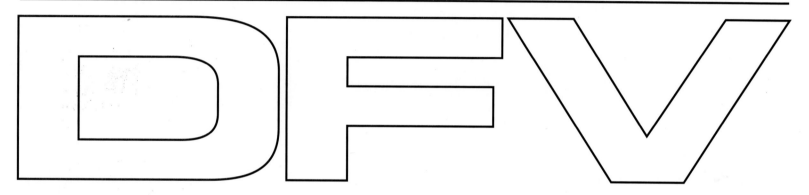

DFV

Haynes Publishing

THE FORD COSWORTH

DFV

The inside story of F1's greatest engine

ANDREW NOAKES

First published in May 2007

A catalogue record for this book is available from the British Library

ISBN 978 1 84425 337 1

Library of Congress control no 2007922000

Published by Haynes Publishing,
Sparkford, Yeovil, Somerset BA22 7JJ, UK
Tel: 01963 442030 Fax: 01963 440001
Int.tel: +44 1963 442030
Int.fax: +44 1963 440001
E-mail: sales@haynes.co.uk
Website: www.haynes.co.uk

Haynes North America Inc.,
861 Lawrence Drive, Newbury Park, California 91320, USA

Design and layout by Nick Moyle

Printed and bound in Britain by J. H. Haynes & Co. Ltd.,
Sparkford, Yeovil, Somerset BA22 7JJ, UK

Photo credits

Alfa Romeo: 105, 126 top
Aston Martin: 22–23, 34,
Audi: 21
Author: 8, 61 bottom, 115 top, 119 top, 139, 142, 176–177, 178, 179, 180, 181, 182, 183
Bentley: 40
BMW: 24, 25, 26–27, 43, 123, 124 top, 126 bottom, 127, 128, 129 top
Classic Team Lotus: 47
DaimlerChrysler: 22 left
Ford: 9, 10–11, 12–13, 14, 15, 18–19, 20, 31, 35, 36, 38–39, 41, 42, 44, 45, 46, 48, 49, 50, 52, 53, 57, 58–59, 60, 61 top, 62, 63, 64, 65, 66, 67, 68, 69, 70, 71, 72–73, 76, 77, 78–79, 81, 82, 83, 84–85, 86, 88, 89, 90, 91, 92, 93, 94, 95, 96, 97, 98, 99, 100, 101, 102, 103, 104, 106, 107 bottom, 108–109, 110, 111, 113, 114, 115 bottom, 116, 117 bottom, 120, 121, 124 bottom, 125, 129 bottom, 130, 131, 134, 135, 136, 137 top, 138 top and middle, 141, 143, 144, 145, 146, 147, 148, 149, 150 top, 151, 152–153, 154, 155, 156, 157, 158, 159, 160, 161, 162, 163, 166, 167, 168, 169, 170, 172, 173
Honda: 30
Ian Wagstaff: 107 top, 137 bottom, 150 bottom
Jaguar: 29 bottom
LAT: 6, 7, 16, 17, 28, 29 top, 32–33, 74, 75, 132–133, 140, 171
Midland Automobile Club: 174
Mirrorpix: 55, 56
Renault: 112, 117 top, 118, 119 bottom, 122
Simon McBeath: 175
Sutton Motosport Images: 164–165
Udo Klinkel: 138 bottom

Author's acknowledgements

Four decades on from the Cosworth DFV's debut in Grand Prix racing, it is sad to note that so many of those who were involved are no longer around to reminisce. My job would have been far easier, and much more enjoyable, if I had been able to talk to Walter Hayes, Colin Chapman, Jim Clark, Graham Hill, Maurice Philippe and, of course, Keith Duckworth, about the part they played in the DFV's success.

Instead, their input into the pages that follow comes only from reports by others, and in some cases from their own written accounts. Rediscovering Denis Jenkinson's tireless reporting of the Grand Prix circus for *Motor Sport* magazine has been one of the great pleasures of compiling a book which deals with one of Formula 1's golden eras. Meanwhile, the memoirs of Stuart Turner, Graham Hill, Andrew Ferguson and Tony Rudd all helped to piece together the DFV story.

In addition, I would like to record particular thanks to: Clive Chapman, Chris Dinnage and Bob Dance of Classic Team Lotus for giving me an insight into the running of a historic F1 operation; Jody Scheckter for finding time in his busy schedule to talk about DFVs and Ferrari flat-12s and provide access to his private race car museum for photography; Stuart McCrudden and Mike Whatley of the Thoroughbred Grand Prix Championship; Patrick Head and Sir Frank Williams of Williams Grand Prix Engineering; John Barnard for details of the DFX and the later part of the DFV's career; Ian Wagstaff and Udo Klinkel for rare photographs from their own collections; Tony May and Mark Joseland of the Midland Automobile Club for hillclimb pictures; Andrew Charman; John Elwin; John Nicholson of Nicholson McLaren Engines; Jim Blackstock, former Cosworth press officer; Mark Wilford and Dave Hill of Ford, and Barry Reynolds, formerly of Ford, for much good advice.

CONTENTS

DFV – THE INSIDE STORY
OF F1'S GREATEST ENGINE

FOREWORD

— BY PATRICK HEAD —

The DFV had about as good a debut as you could wish for – pole position, fastest lap and first across the line. Keith Duckworth had spent many 18-hour days at his drawing board, which didn't do his eyesight much good, but the engine he produced proved its quality straight away. Soon it was dominating the Formula 1 grids.

In 1974, when I went to work with Ron Tauranac at Trojan, the DFV was already eight years old with more than 50 Grand Prix wins to its credit. Because Keith had got the basic design right and had ensured that the production engineering was sorted out, it was still a reliable and competitive engine. At the time it was the only engine a privateer team could sensibly consider.

Tauranac persuaded Trojan's owner, Peter Agg, that they could adapt their Formula 5000 car to do a Formula 1 season for very little money. The result was the not very superb T103, a rather ugly car with Tauranac's then-trademark nose with two radiators at the front and a wing in the middle like the 'lobster claw' Brabham. It was powered, of course, by a Ford Cosworth DFV engine.

We started Williams Grand Prix Engineering in 1977, and all our early cars were powered by DFVs. After a year running a March we moved on to our own FW06, and then the 'ground effect' FW07. We ran DFV-powered cars until 1983, winning 17 Grands Prix, two drivers' championships (with Alan Jones and Keke Rosberg) and back-to-back constructors' titles in 1980 and 1981.

By then the Renault turbo engine was becoming more and more powerful, and Ferrari were going turbo, and we realised that we were going to have difficulty being competitive with the DFV. Cosworth responded with DFV upgrades and we started our own development programme with John Judd at Engine Developments.

For 1984 we switched to Honda turbo engines. Keith spent a long time campaigning against the turbo engines, and it was a shame he didn't just get on and design one. Ironically, in America Larry Slutter at Parnelli

Jones Racing developed the DFV into a very successful turbocharged engine for IndyCar racing. Keith was always quite contemptuous of chassis people fiddling with his engine, but he could see that America was a whole new market. Cosworth adopted the turbo engine and called it the DFX.

The pages that follow tell the story of a quite brilliant engine, which was almost completely designed by Keith Duckworth himself. It was a remarkable achievement, and the DFV's phenomenally long and successful career is never likely to be equalled.

Patrick Head
Director of Engineering
WilliamsF1
Grove, Oxfordshire

INTRODUCTION

When Jim Clark's Lotus 49 crossed the finishing line at Zandvoort on 4 June 1967 to win the DFV engine's first Grand Prix, it marked the beginning of a remarkable era in Formula 1 racing. It was an era in which the DFV would come to dominate Grand Prix grids, and would power more than 150 race winners and nine World Champion drivers. More than that, it was an era when a team without the resources of Ferrari, BRM or Honda could build its own car, buy a competitive engine off the shelf, and win races. It levelled the field, and made F1 racing ever more competitive and more exciting.

It is a remarkable story. Not just because of the DFV engine's long career and its impressive tally of race victories, and not only because it also powered Le Mans winners and hillclimb champions and Tasman cars, and 152 winners of IndyCar races. The DFV's tale is also a fascinating story of the persistence and tenacity of Colin Chapman, who found the funding to develop it in the first place. It's the story of Keith Duckworth's genius in creating a tough, powerful engine that could win straight out of the box and go on winning for years to come. And it's the story of the designers, the drivers – and the rivals – who turned the DFV era into one of the most exciting in the history of motor sport.

It was an era which would see enormous strides in aerodynamic performance, in tyre technology, in materials technology and, eventually, in engine design. Even then, when the DFV had been driven out of F1 by turbo engines, it would return for a final encore before technology rushed towards the future and left it behind for good.

The stories and the achievements in the pages that follow, the victories and failures, the losses and the laughs, are a tribute to one of the greatest engines of all time – and to the people who created it.

The most successful engine in F1 history: the Duckworth-designed DFV (left) won 155 World Championship Grand Prix, the first of them at Zandvoort in 1967 (right).

CHAPTER ONE

DUCKWORTH, COSTIN AND THE BIRTH OF COSWORTH

Keith Duckworth and Mike Costin were very different, and yet they made a remarkable team, a team that produced a string of very effective racing engines and the most successful Formula 1 engine in the history of the sport. Duckworth was the great thinker, the constant innovator who solved problems by working from first principles. Costin was the practical, hands-on engineer and development driver with an instinctive understanding of what worked and what didn't. Each provided the ideal foil for the other, and between them they set up Cosworth Engineering, a company which would become renowned for engineering excellence and would be the power for countless victories in a bewildering range of racing categories.

Both developed early interests in mechanical things, but neither of Cosworth's founders was from an engineering background. Duckworth was born in 1933 in Blackburn, Lancashire, where his father owned a weaving shed and traded cloth at the Manchester Cotton Exchange. His grandfather provided the family's only motor sport connection, as he had taken part in competition before the First World War. Young Keith was a keen constructor of model engines and aircraft, building his first rubber-band-powered aeroplane at the age of eight and soon moving on to radio-controlled

The first win for a Cosworth-Ford engine: Jim Clark's Lotus 18 Formula Junior car takes the flag at Goodwood in March 1960.

MWC 884C

models, for which he built his own radio equipment. His enthusiasm was rewarded when his father bought a collection of machine tools and installed them in what had been the air-raid shelter at the back of the house. Duckworth taught himself how to operate all the machines, and used them to make parts for his steam engines and model aircraft.

Duckworth attended schools in Blackburn until he was nine years old and then went to Giggleswick School, following in the footsteps of his older brother, Brian. At the age of 18 he was called up into the RAF, where he trained as a pilot on de Havilland Chipmunks and twin-engined Airspeed Oxfords. After a flying misdemeanour he was sent off to Portsmouth to train as a navigator instead, and he flew numerous training missions in Avro Ansons. At the end of his two years of National Service, in 1952, Duckworth left the RAF and enrolled at Imperial College, London to study for a degree in mechanical engineering. It was there that he first became interested in motorsport, and he spent many a weekend at nearby racing circuits – Goodwood in Sussex, Brands Hatch in Kent and Silverstone in Northamptonshire.

The motor racing bug had clearly bitten deeply, because in 1953, Duckworth decided to buy a Lotus Six sports/racing car kit powered by a 1.1-litre Coventry Climax engine. The Climax was the most expensive of the engine options, and Duckworth built up the kit using the best new parts wherever possible. When the Lotus was complete he drove it in a handful of races, but quickly concluded that he was not cut out to be a racing driver. Later, he would spend a summer vacation working at the tiny workshops in Hornsey where Lotus was then based, and in 1957 Colin Chapman offered him a full-time job as a gearbox development engineer. It was at Lotus that Duckworth would first work alongside his future partner, Mike Costin.

Costin was born in London in 1929, the third of four children. His father was a marbler and grainer whose painting skills were much in demand among the well-to-do between the wars. Like Duckworth, Costin's early years were heavily influenced by aircraft, largely because of his brother Frank's interest. Frank Costin would later become an engineer in the aircraft industry, and would use his knowledge of aerodynamics to design low-drag bodywork for racing cars – including some early Lotuses, and the famous 'teardrop' Vanwall. Mike left school before his 16th birthday, and went to the de Havilland aircraft company in Hatfield on a trade apprenticeship as

Cosworth's early fortunes were largely tied to a new, short-stroke 997cc engine introduced in the Ford Anglia in 1959. It provided the basis for Cosworth engines which won in Formula Junior, Formula 3 and Formula 2.

Ford developed a strong relationship with Cosworth, which productionised the Lotus-Ford Twin Cam and then built tuned versions for the works Lotus-Cortinas. This is Jim Clark, in characteristic pose.

and finally concluded that the gears needed to be wider, which meant spending money on casting a new, larger gearbox casing. When Chapman refused on cost grounds, Duckworth stood by his principles – and left the company.

Duckworth and Costin had already realised they worked well together, and they had hatched a plan to set up in business together, offering design and development services for motor racing folk. Combining the 'Cos' of Costin and the 'worth' of Duckworth, they came up with the businesslike name Cosworth, and the company was officially born at the end of September 1958. Costin had just signed a new, three-year contract with Lotus (no doubt because Chapman had got wind of the Duckworth/Costin partnership and wanted to hang onto his Technical Director for a while longer), so in the earliest days of the new company it was effectively a one-man operation, although Duckworth's wife Ursula helped out. At first Duckworth shared a garage in Shaftesbury Mews, London W8, but soon the nascent Cosworth organisation moved to some old stables in Friern Barnet, North London, where Duckworth installed his first major machinery purchase – a dynamometer for testing engines.

Cosworth's early work was varied. Duckworth prepared racing cars, and rebuilt Coventry Climax engines for the racing Lotus Elites of Ian Walker and Graham Warner's Chequered Flag team. Cosworth also built engines for Elva racing cars, and made components such as suspension wishbones. Much of the machining work was farmed out to a machine shop called Rood's Engineering in Walthamstow. Rood's would later be absorbed into the growing Cosworth business, and proprietor Ben Rood would become a Cosworth director.

In 1959, Duckworth started to prepare a Formula Junior car for Howard Panton, a friend from his college days. The rules demanded modified production engines, either with a 1,000cc capacity limit in cars weighing at least 360kg or a 1,100cc limit in cars weighing at least 400kg. The Fiat 1100 engine was already a popular choice for Formula Junior cars but Panton, who was now working for Ford, knew the short-stroke 105E Anglia engine was about to be released and that seemed like a much better basis for a racing engine. Duckworth got hold of a couple of these promising new engines to work on.

Early problems with camshafts were solved by application of what would become the classic

a fitter. After two years at de Havilland he was 'upgraded' into an engineering apprenticeship which provided training in a wider range of subjects. At the end of his apprenticeship Costin, like Duckworth, joined the RAF for his two-year National Service, then in 1951 he rejoined de Havilland as a design draughtsman. It was while he was still working at de Havilland that Costin met Colin Chapman through a mutual friend, Peter Ross, and agreed to start working part-time for Lotus while still retaining his day job. By the mid-1950s Costin had left de Havilland to work full-time at Lotus, under the imposing title of Technical Director, and he had also started racing Lotus cars with considerable success.

Less successful was the project which Chapman had given to Keith Duckworth on his arrival at Lotus – development of a new five-speed gearbox which had been designed by Richard Ansdale. Duckworth stepped into the shoes of one Graham Hill, who was in the process of swapping his career as an engineer for a more successful one as a professional racing driver. The new gearbox was tiny, and very light, but so far had proved frustratingly unreliable. It had already acquired the nickname 'Queerbox'. Duckworth spent 10 months trying to build reliability into the design,

Duckworth method – throw the book away and think hard about everything, from first principles. New cam designs allowed the engine to rev harder and provided Cosworth with a competitive 80bhp power unit, which made its debut at the 1959 Boxing Day meeting at Brands Hatch. Before long Formula Junior business was booming for Cosworth, and the company had outgrown its workshops in the old stables at Friern Barnet. Cosworth moved to Edmonton, where it took over workshops just vacated by Lotus. Late in 1962 Mike Costin finally arrived at Cosworth full-time.

In the early 1960s, Cosworth continued building successful racing engines, and also began to perform contract work for road car projects. One early job for Ford, which received very little publicity, was to design and develop the Cortina GT 'semi-circular' inlet manifold and Weber carburettor installation, along with the GT cam profile. Cosworth also productionised the Harry Mundy/Richard Ansdale-designed Lotus-Ford Twin Cam engine, and then set about developing race-tuned Twin Cams for the works Lotus-Cortina race and rally cars.

The next major project for Cosworth was to build engines for the new Formula 3, which would be replacing Formula Junior for 1964, and for the new 1.0-litre Formula 2, which had much less restrictive rules than F3. The Formula 3 unit still had to be based on a production engine, and had to be fed by just one, single-choke carburettor. Cosworth's answer was the MAE – Modified Anglia Engine – which was a comprehensive update of the existing twin-Weber Formula Junior unit. Despite the handicap of a single carburettor choke, Duckworth soon had a 10,000rpm production-based engine developing 100bhp/litre.

For Formula 2, Duckworth embarked on a much more ambitious plan. The short-stroke Ford 116E bottom end would be retained, but Cosworth would fit a new purpose-built light alloy cylinder head, complete with an overhead camshaft. The new engine would be called the SCA, which stood for 'Single Cam – Series A', and funding for its development came directly from Ford, which had taken note of Cosworth's Formula Junior successes with Ford-based engines. A budget of £17,500 was allocated for the design and development of the new power unit.

The SCA's new overhead camshaft was driven by a gear train from the front of the crankshaft, and operated eight in-line valves which were fed by efficient, steeply angled ports. Duckworth was keen to avoid the 'shrouding' effect of a conventional bathtub combustion chamber, where the wall of the chamber reduces the gas flow through the ports. Enlarging the chamber to reduce the shrouding effect lowers the compression ratio, which is not an option for a race engine. Instead, Duckworth avoided shrouding by forming Heron-type combustion chambers in the piston crowns by machining valve cut-outs into them. Volumetric efficiency was excellent because, for the greater part of the piston stroke, there was nothing to shroud the valves and limit gas flow. But the SCA had its problems, the main one being poor combustion. Cosworth eventually found that the SCA worked best with 49 degrees of ignition advance, indicating that combustion was slow.

Even so, the Cosworth SCA was the Formula 2 engine to beat in 1964 and 1965, winning the championship in both years. It was still competitive into 1966, but eventually was overtaken by Honda's very special four-valve engine. By then, Duckworth was working on his own four-valve unit, the FVA, for the new 1.6-litre Formula 2 which was due to come into force in 1967. That engine, of course, was to play a major role in the development of the DFV.

Harry Mundy and Richard Ansdale designed the Lotus-Ford Twin Cam engine, but it was Cosworth's detail engineering which turned it into a reliable production engine.

EARLY DAYS AT LOTUS

If Cosworth provided the engine design know-how behind the DFV, Lotus provided the impetus.

Colin Chapman created the first Lotus in 1948, an Austin 7 special with boxed-in chassis rails and a marine-ply body, which he used as a trials car. In 1949, he moved on to the Ford-engined Lotus Mk2, which he raced the following year with considerable success. The Mk3 Lotus was even more successful, becoming almost unbeatable in the 750 Motor Club Championship. It was this car which featured Chapman's famous 'de-siamesed' ports, created using a fabricated inlet manifold which projected into the ports in the block to improve gas flow.

The Lotus Engineering Company was officially founded in 1952. After several more Austin 7-based cars, Chapman created the Mk6 with a brand-new steel-tube chassis, and this became the first 'production' Lotus. It was usually supplied in kit form, for the customer to complete. A succession of increasingly ambitious sports-racing cars followed. In 1955, Chapman's chassis design expertise was sufficiently well recognised for him to be approached by Tony Vandervell to redesign the Vanwall chassis, and Chapman's design went on to win the first ever F1 constructor's title in 1958. By then Lotus was in Formula 2 and Formula 1 with the Type 12, and at end of 1959 the company had grown so much that it needed a new factory, which was purpose built on Delamare Road, Cheshunt. There the company made its first real road car, the glassfibre monocoque Type 14 Elite.

Lotus won its first F1 races with

Cliff Allison on the way to a fourth-place finish in the 1958 Belgian Grand Prix at Spa in his Lotus 12 Climax.

the mid-engined Type 18 in 1960, followed by the much smaller and sleeker Type 21 in 1961. For 1962 Chapman presented customers with the spaceframe Lotus 24, but for the works team he schemed the Type 25, with a 'bath tub' stressed-skin chassis which was both lighter and stiffer. Jim Clark looked set to win the World Championship in 1962, but lost out to Graham Hill in the BRM when an oil leak caused his retirement from the final race of the season. Clark retaliated in 1963, winning a record seven Grands Prix in a season and running away with the championship. In the Type 25 and evolutionary Type 33, Clark won three more races in 1964, but a string of engine failures left him third in the championship. In 1965, he won every race he finished – six of them – and ran away with the world title for a second time.

Lotus was now not just a championship-winning race car constructor, it was also a growing car manufacturer and a profitable business. But even greater achievements were still to come.

Lotus started out as a competition car manufacturer, its first true road car being the Elite in 1959.

CHAPTER TWO

F1'S NEW ERA

It's easy to think of the early days of Grand Prix
motor racing at the beginning of the 20th century as
the preserve of enormous, agricultural cars powered
by low-revving engines with cylinders the size of
dustbins, piloted by heroes in cloth helmets and
unencumbered by the restrictive and ever-changing
regulations that shape the modern sport. Some of
that, of course, is true, but blaming the governance of
modern motor sport for the epidemic of rule changes
is to over-simplify the history of racing. Changing and
developing regulations have been a part of the sport
since its inception.

Motorsport's governing body, the sporting
commission (Commission Sportive International, or CSI)
of the Federation Internationale de l'Automobile (FIA),
announced a new set of regulations in October 1958.
This was the twelfth major change in the rules since
Grand Prix racing had been given its first true structure
in 1906. In the half-century since then, rule changes
had restricted engines to 4.5-litres, then to 3.0-litres,
2.0-litres and finally 1.5-litres. Engines had been
de-restricted, and then re-restricted. Minimum weight
limits had been introduced to ensure the cars were
not too flimsy, then abolished to encourage more
competitors, and then replaced by rules limiting the
maximum weight of the car, which it was thought
would limit engine size. Equalisation formulas between
supercharged and unsupercharged engines had been
introduced, changed, and changed again.

Since 1954, Formula 1 rules had required 2.5-litre
normally aspirated engines or 'blown' 750cc units,
although few took the forced-induction option seriously.
British constructors had achieved a great deal of success

*McLaren's M2B was often unreliable during 1966 – seen
here at Monaco. After problems with the Ford engine
McLaren tried a Serenissima V8, but soon switched back to
the Ford – but in Mexico it let him down again.*

LEFT: *Auto Union's mid-engined cars of the 1930s were way ahead of their time. At their peak, the supercharged engines produced over 500bhp, a power output which would not be seen again in Formula 1 until the turbo era of the 1980s.*

under these rules, first by perfecting the conventional front-engined car (Vanwall, BRM P25) and then by innovating with lighter, nimbler rear-engined machinery (Cooper, Lotus, BRM P48). The new formula announced in 1958, and due to come into force for the 1961 season, stipulated 1.5-litre unsupercharged engines – the same size as the existing Formula 2. The engines were required to run on pump fuel (not the exotic methanol fuels that were the norm until 1958) and they powered cars with a minimum dry weight of 450kg (992lb). In Britain there was outrage. Many felt the regulations changes were being introduced specifically to bring Britain's run of success to an end.

Howls of protest at the new formula were accompanied by a concerted effort to keep the 2.5-litre cars running, by organising a number of non-championship races for the larger-engined cars. 'The British took the attitude that if we ignored it, it would go away. It did not,' recalled BRM designer Tony Rudd in his autobiography *It Was Fun!* 'By mid-1960 it was clear not only was it going to happen, but Ferrari was good and ready and Porsche was not far away.' Too late the British teams realised that their 'Intercontinental Formula' for 3.0-litre cars, which they had proposed as an alternative to the 1.5-litre Formula 1, was not going to generate the expected interest among American teams and would have no support from Continental manufacturers. That left it as little more than a footnote to the more

OPPOSITE: *The 2.7-litre Alfa Romeo P3 of 1932 was the first genuine single-seater Grand Prix car. It humbled the Mercedes and Auto Union opposition at the German Grand Prix in 1935, with Tazio Nuvolari at the wheel.*

glamorous business of Grand Prix racing, even if the 'Intercontinental' cars were faster and potentially more spectacular. Indeed, the reduction in speeds that would result from the move to 1.5-litre engines for Grand Prix cars was increasingly seen as desirable and responsible, coming as it did after a tragic season in which three Formula 1 drivers – Luigi Musso, Peter Collins and Stuart Lewis-Evans – had been lost in racing accidents.

Belatedly, development of British engines for the new 1.5-litre formula got underway. While both Coventry Climax and BRM busily schemed new small-capacity V8s, Coventry Climax readied a stopgap 1.5-litre version of its Formula 2 FPF four-cylinder engine, which was effectively one bank of the unraced 2.5-litre FPE 'Godiva' V8 which the company had designed for Formula 1 back in 1952. Even BRM, which had always built its own engines and often made even the smallest components in preference to buying them in from outside suppliers, was forced to fit Climax FPFs to its mid-engined P57s while its own V8 was under development. Both British V8s would appear late in 1961, the Coventry Climax FWMV in August and the BRM P57 in September, but neither engine would be a race-winning package until 1962. For most of the 1961 season Ferrari's shark-nose

156s with their wide-angle V6s had things their own way, winning five of the eight World Championship races.

But if the introduction of the 1.5-litre formula really had been an attempt to nullify the British challenge, the effects would not last long. In 1962, BRM's V8 powered Graham Hill to victory in the championship, narrowly beating Jim Clark in Colin Chapman's monocoque Lotus 25. The following year, Clark won a record seven races in the Climax V8-powered Lotus to take his first World Championship. Ferrari's John Surtees won two races and pipped Graham Hill to the world title by a point in 1964, but it was Hill, Clark and Brabham-Climax driver Dan Gurney who headed the lap charts for the bulk of the season. Clark was back on top in 1965, winning six more Grands Prix to bring the drivers' and constructors' titles back to Lotus. The diversity of F1 technology was underlined by Ferrari's trial of a flat-12 as an alternative to its V8s and V6s, Porsche's air-cooled flat-8 and Honda's high-revving transverse V12, alongside the British V8s.

Despite on-track dramas and some good racing, there was soon widespread dissatisfaction with the 1.5-litre formula. Formula 1 was supposed to be the pinnacle of the sport, the ultimate in speed and spectacle – yet the new generation of mid-engined sports prototypes, like Ferrari's 4.4-litre 365P, Lola's Chevrolet-engined T70 and McLaren's Ford-powered M1A were thundering around Europe's tracks in lap times that matched F1 cars. And they were spectacular: such was the level of roadholding generated by the latest mid-engined Formula 1 cars that they seemed to 'corner on rails'. The FIA sought the views of the F1 competitors in 1963 before deciding on a replacement formula for 1966, and the Lotus, BRM, Cooper and Brabham teams, along with engine manufacturer Coventry Climax and Dean Delamont of the RAC, all travelled to Paris for a meeting with the FIA's sporting commission, the CSI. Privately, the teams were agreed that a 2.0-litre formula would be ideal, making the cars faster and more exciting but allowing the use of stretched versions of existing engines. Experience had shown that the FIA tended to negotiate downwards from whatever they proposed, so the teams decided to start negotiating at 3.0 litres. However, the meeting with the FIA didn't quite go to plan.

Colin Chapman spoke on behalf of the assembled constructors and engine men, and made his case for a 3.0-litre formula. The FIA immediately accepted. As BRM's Tony Rudd recalled: 'That was that. We filed out,

Jack Brabham (left) and John Cooper had the measure of the front-engined Ferraris in 1959 and 1960.

John Cooper's 'victory rolls' became a familiar sight in the final years of the 2.5-litre formula. Here he celebrates another Brabham win.

to about £15 million today) but beyond that racing had absorbed an enormous amount of time and resource which had taken its toll on the company's more profitable mainstream work.

To keep the FWMV V8 competitive Coventry Climax was continually working on detail changes: wider bores, a flat-plane crankshaft with a shorter stroke, new low-line exhausts and ultimately, four-valve cylinder heads with twin camshafts driven by a geartrain instead of a chain. Power climbed to around 210bhp at 10,500rpm. In addition, Walter Hassan and Peter Windsor-Smith had begun work on a completely new 1.5-litre engine, the flat-16 FWMW, which was expected to give 240bhp at 12,000rpm. Four FWMW engines were built, but the project never progressed beyond the prototype stage as the Climax V8s continued to be successful – and in any case, by then the end of the 1.5-litre formula was in sight. The flat-16 never even got as far as installation in a car, although Lotus had readied a single Type 39 with a truncated monocoque tub and tubular engine subframe to carry it. That car was instead fitted with a 2.5-litre Climax FPF and raced in Australia and New Zealand in the Tasman series.

Inevitably, much speculation now centred around the 3.0-litre engines that were being developed for the new formula. The pursuit of maximum power left engine designers searching for the optimum combination of piston area and engine speed. Multi-cylinder engines were the answer: smaller cylinders in greater numbers can increase piston area for a given engine capacity, and if intelligently designed will reduce internal stresses and allow higher safe rev limits. With good breathing and control of frictional losses, high revs bring a high power output. Ferrari led the trend by discarding its V6 in favour of a V12, a configuration it had not used in F1 since 1951. The engine was a revamped version of its 312 sports car unit, reduced from 3.3 litres to 3.0 litres. Although sports car racing was now a high priority at Ferrari – to the detriment of the F1 campaign, some said – the team seemed as well prepared for the start of the 3.0-litre formula as it had been when 1.5-litre engines were introduced five years earlier. The Maranello team was the pre-season favourite.

At BRM, Tony Rudd had put the painful memories of the unsuccessful 1.5-litre V16 of 1951 behind him and was scheming a new 16-cylinder engine – this time a twin-crankshaft H16. Rudd reasoned that such an engine could be built by taking two of the team's successful 1.5-litre V8s, opening out the V-angle to form flat-8s, and

absolutely thunderstruck… Wally [Hassan, of Coventry Climax] said: "You've done it now, I don't think I can get the funds for a 3.0-litre".'

Racing had always been a promotional activity for Coventry Climax, one that had been driven by the personal interest of chairman Sir Leonard Lee, son of company founder H. Pulham Lee. Coventry Climax earned its bread and butter building engines that powered fire pumps and motivated a whole cottage industry of specialist sports cars between the wars and later it designed and manufactured its own range of fork-lift trucks. The first sign of financial pressures on Coventry Climax's racing activities came in October 1962, when Sir Leonard Lee announced the company's withdrawal from racing – a decision he rescinded when Lotus, Cooper, Lola and other Climax customers managed to squeeze more out of the fuel and tyre companies sponsoring them. Racing continued even after the takeover of Coventry Climax in 1963 by William Lyons's successful Jaguar company, which had already taken control of Daimler in 1960, but the rising costs of developing competitive engines continued to come under close scrutiny. Estimates put the direct costs of Climax's racing activities at up to £1 million (equivalent

laying one on top of the other with their crankshafts geared together. The benefits went far further than the simple convenience of doubling up the 1.5-litre capacity to make a 3.0-litre engine. More importantly, it meant that the new engine would benefit from the well-developed combustion chamber, cylinder geometry and valve gear which had proved successful in the V8. Originally, the two banks of cylinders on each side of the engine were to share a single inlet camshaft, but that idea was dropped and the H16 raced with four exhaust cams and four inlets. It first ran in February 1966, and developed 410bhp at 10,500rpm – though it was heavy and reliability was suspect.

Cooper had a ready-made source of engines thanks to its new owners, Jonathan Sieff's Chipstead Motor Group, which handled Maserati sales in the UK. Speculation in *Motoring News* that Cooper's 3.0-litre F1 machine would be powered by *two* 1.5-litre Maserati V12s proved predictably wide of the mark. Instead, Giulio Alfieri dusted off a Maserati V12 which had first been used in F1 in 1957 in 2.5-litre form, and then turned into a big-bore 3.0-litre sports car unit. By enlarging the bores still further and cutting the stroke, Alfieri arrived at a 3.0-litre V12 good for 10,000rpm. With twin gear-

ABOVE: *Tony Rudd's beautifully neat P261 was one of the most successful 1.5-litre cars, and with 2.0-litre 'Tasman' engines it continued to win at the start of the 3.0-litre era.*

LEFT: *Walter Hassan was the technical driving force behind Coventry Climax in Formula 1. It was the company's withdrawal from racing in 1965 which prompted the development of the DFV engine.*

driven overhead camshafts on each cylinder bank, twin ignition with a pair of 12-plug distributors, and Lucas fuel injection, it generated around 360bhp – enough to win races. Further development saw a third valve and even a third spark plug squeezed into a crowded combustion chamber, but to no significant effect. Also ineffective was a Cooper-based special with an ATS sports car V8, briefly used by Jo Bonnier and later taken over by Silvio Moser, and a 1964 Cooper chassis into which a Ferrari 250GT engine was shoehorned.

Dan Gurney's new All-American Racers team fitted its Eagle cars with 2.7-litre Climax FPF units, which had been developed for Cooper's 1961 Indianapolis effort, while a new V12 was readied by Harry Weslake at Rye. Bruce McLaren's brand-new M2B Formula 1 cars debuted with a 3.0-litre version of the big Ford V8 which had been used in IndyCar racing, then switched to the Serenissima V8 which proved unreliable. A more outlandish effort came from Paul Emery, who unearthed the old 2.5-litre Coventry Climax FPE V8 from the mid-'50s, adapted it to run on regulation pump fuel and added Tecalemit fuel injection. It was installed in a new chassis designed by Hugh Aiden-Jones and known as the Shannon Mk1. Ex-Lotus driver Trevor Taylor was

engaged, and the Shannon was entered for the British Grand Prix at Brands Hatch in 1966 where it qualified 18th and managed half a lap before the fuel tank split. It never graced F1 again, giving Shannon the shortest Grand Prix career of any marque…

While some rumours circulated that Coventry Climax was working on a new V8, an update of the 2.5-litre FPE V8 from 1954, others reckoned the Climax engine for the 3.0-litre formula would be a flat-16 like the stillborn 1.5-litre FWMW. But in February 1965 Coventry Climax quashed all the speculation by announcing that its motor racing operation would be wound up at the end of the 1965 season. There would be no 3.0-litre engine from the Coventry manufacturer. 'Once we had made our decision to pull out, and informed the constructors and the press, we planned a clean break,' explains Climax technical director Wally Hassan in his autobiography *Climax in Coventry*. 'Peter Windsor-Smith and I never even got around to sketching out 3-litre layouts, although we had a very clear idea of the sort of engine we would have designed.' Hassan rebuffed ideas of supercharging the 1.5-litre FWMV or even the FWMW flat-16: 'The approaches all came from people who were hoping they would not have to buy all-new engines, or to build all-new cars… I was quite convinced we could not do the job properly, and advised against it.'

Teams that had so far relied on Climax power – Lotus, Cooper, and Jack Brabham's up-and-coming eponymous outfit – would all have to find a new source of engines. For Brabham the solution lay in Australia, with help almost incidentally from the Detroit-based giant, General Motors. Australian automotive parts supplier Repco had diversified into motorsport, building Climax FPF engines for the Australia/New Zealand Tasman racing series. Given a suitable block, Brabham decided, Repco might be willing to build a 3.0-litre F1 engine. After examining alloy blocks in Japan and America, Brabham found a lightweight road-car block of about the right size – from the Oldsmobile F85 of 1961–63. Although the engine had just been discontinued (GM turned to thin-wall iron blocks which were only a little heavier, and much cheaper to make) supplies of the cylinder blocks were still easy to find.

Repco engaged Phil Irving, of Vincent motorcycle fame, as a consultant and set about transforming the pushrod Oldsmobile V8 by adding a single chain-driven overhead camshaft on each cylinder bank, dry-sump lubrication and a flat-plane crankshaft machined from an EN40 steel billet by Laystall. With Lucas fuel injection the

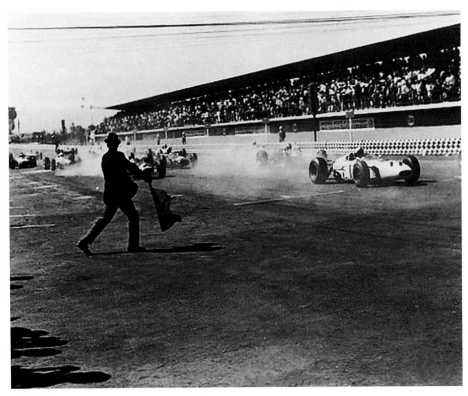

The day the Climaxes failed: Richie Ginther takes the starter's flag for Honda's first F1 victory, in Mexico in October 1965. None of the top Climax and BRM-engined cars finished, and the flat-12 Ferraris were well beaten.

Brabham-Repco RB620 developed 285bhp at 7,500rpm on its first dynamometer runs in March 1965 and by 1966 it was almost up to 300bhp. While other 3.0-litre engines would soon produce more power, the Brabham-Repco V8 would have simplicity and reliability on its side. More importantly it would be ready to race at the very beginning of the new Formula 1 season, at the non-championship South African Grand Prix on 1 January 1966, where it would lead comfortably until the drive belt to the fuel-injection unit failed.

Colin Chapman's approach to the power problem was, predictably, more ambitious. Clearly, a new engine, purpose-built for the 3.0-litre formula, was the optimum solution. Cosworth's solid relationship with Lotus in lower racing formulas, and Keith Duckworth's ability to create race-winning engines, made the choice of engine designer an easy one. Simple, too, was the choice of strategy for designing the engine. The FIA's changes to the racing formulas included a new, 1.6-litre Formula 2, due to appear in 1967. Duckworth saw no reason why a four-cylinder F2 engine of 1.6 litres should not be doubled up into a V8 of around 3.0 litres. Much more difficult was the task of arranging finance for the development of a new engine. Duckworth's

rule-of-thumb calculations, based on the design and construction of the F2 engine and then the F1 unit, suggested a budget of £100,000 would be necessary.

This was an era when sponsorship was still specifically banned in Formula 1; remember: the sport ran on money from tyre and oil companies, spark-plug manufacturers, and the like. Evidence of these trade sponsors' support came only in discreet patches on the drivers' overalls and much less discreet full-page press ads when their cars won. BRM and Ferrari raced for glory which reflected well on other areas of their businesses, just as Coventry Climax had until the costs became too great to bear. Smaller independents like Lotus relied on outside support, and developing an expensive new engine meant finding a rich partner to help.

Chapman approached the Society of Motor Manufacturers and Traders (SMMT), the body which represented the British motor industry, with a persuasive argument: Coventry Climax's withdrawal from racing was a disaster for the British motor industry's prestige on the world stage, and what was needed was a new Formula 1 engine backed by the industry as a whole. The SMMT sympathised, but representations to the Wilson Labour government of the time came to nothing. The

Bruce McLaren's new team used a 3.0-litre version of the Ford Indy V8 in its M2B Formula 1 car, a much larger and heavier engine than Duckworth had in mind.

SMMT's president, Patrick Hennessy, was also chairman of Ford of Britain, and although Ford was already heavily involved with Lotus in touring car racing and Indy racing, the company declined the opportunity to enter Formula 1. Negotiations with sports car manufacturer Aston Martin also fell through. Aston Martin owner David Brown was enthusiastic, but wanted more control over the project than either Chapman or Duckworth would have been happy with. As Chapman told motor racing author Doug Nye, Brown 'virtually wanted to buy Cosworth'. Keith Duckworth approached Geoff Murdoch of Esso, supplier of fuel, oil and much of the working capital for the Lotus F1 team, while Chapman spoke to Dr Daniel McDonald of the hugely successful BSR record turntable company based in the Midlands, but neither meeting came to anything.

Even if a suitable benefactor could be found, the process of designing and developing a Grand Prix engine could be expected to take a year or more, leaving Lotus engineless for the 1966 season. Officially, Coventry Climax had withdrawn from racing, but Chapman persuaded the company to build him two engines for 1966 – stretched versions of the FWMV V8 and known as the Mark IX. By mating the 72.39mm bore of the 1965 engine with the original long-stroke (60mm) crankshaft from 1961 the V8's capacity was increased from 1,497cc to 1,974cc, and at the same time its power output rose from 213bhp to 240bhp. 'We felt able to help Jim Clark in the interim because, along with Coventry Climax, he and Lotus had won a remarkable number of events under the old 1.5-litre rules,' recalls Walter Hassan in *Climax in Coventry*. 'There was, however, very little development involved in this "interim" engine… once they were built we did no further development.'

Even so, the 2.0-litre FWMV was good enough to keep the Lotus 33s in the hunt on twistier tracks, and it would prove to be a successful package in Tasman racing. But it still left Lotus uncompetitive on the faster Grand Prix circuits where top-end power was essential. With only a 2.0-litre V8, Lotus would be at a significant disadvantage compared with the 3.0-litre cars of Brabham, BRM and Ferrari. In July 1965, Chapman solved this problem, and raised a few eyebrows in the process, by striking a deal with old rivals BRM for supplies of their powerful, if heavy, H16 engine. Len Terry, designer of the 33, had left Lotus to design Eagles for Dan Gurney, so it was his replacement, Maurice Philippe, who penned a new chassis to take the H16. In fact, Philippe worked on two related cars, the Type 43 F1 and the Type 42

Honda's 3.0-litre RA273 made its debut at Monza in 1966, in the hands of Richie Ginther. The Honda V12 was probably the most powerful of all the early 3.0-litre F1 engines.

Indianapolis machine, the latter intended to use a 4.2-litre version of the H16, which never materialised, so the car was given a quad-cam Ford V8 instead. Significantly, though both cars were given stressed-skin monocoque structures which had much in common with the Len Terry-designed Lotus 38 Indy car, they were designed as 'truncated' monocoques.

The 38 had chassis members to support the engine and rear suspension, but in Philippe's 42 and 43 the main tub ended in a 360-degree stressed fuel tank section behind the driver's shoulders, and the bulky H16 was bolted to the back to act as the rear part of the structure. BRM's Tony Rudd had always intended the H16 to be a stressed member, and used it that way in his own Type 83 and Type 115 cars. Most of the rear suspension loads were fed through a lower wishbone into the crankcase and gearbox casing. The cast wheel hub carriers were extended upwards to meet a lateral top link on each side, the inner ends of these links being carried on the cylinder heads. Long radius rods were spaced wide apart to clear the side induction boxes of the H16 engine, and picked up on mounting points at the top and bottom corners of the tub itself. In construction, and weight, the Lotus 43 was more Indy

than F1, but at least it promised the power necessary for Lotus to keep up on the faster circuits.

With the immediate engine supply problem solved, Chapman pressed ahead with his plan for the future – a new engine. The Lotus boss pursued a variety of more or less interested parties, and spared none of his industry contacts. One of them was Walter Hayes, former editor of the *Sunday Dispatch* newspaper, for which he had engaged Chapman to write a motoring column. In 1962 Hayes had joined Ford of Britain as director of public affairs. Hayes's remit also included Ford's competition activities, and it hadn't been long before Chapman and Hayes had orchestrated a high-performance Cortina project, the Lotus-Cortina, for race, rally and road use. Hayes soon knew Keith Duckworth and Cosworth as suppliers of tuned twin-cam engines for works Lotus-Cortinas, and would later provide financial backing for Cosworth's most ambitious project yet – the Ford-based Formula 2 SCA engine.

'I sometimes used to go round to Colin's house in Hadley Wood, for dinner, and a chat,' Hayes later recounted to Graham Robson in *Cosworth – The Search For Power*. 'On one occasion he said to me: "This is getting serious, I don't suppose you would do an engine, would you?"' Fortunately for Chapman, Hayes had been toying with the idea of building a Ford Grand Prix engine in-house, to build on the success of the Ford-based Cosworth SCA in Formula 2. The idea of bankrolling an engine for Lotus, to be designed by Duckworth, was an appealing alternative. Hayes discussed the idea with Harley Copp, Vice President of Engineering for Ford of Britain, who had recently arrived from Dearborn. Copp turned out to be a big motorsport enthusiast, and soon Chapman was invited to make his case. For £100,000, his impassioned plea went, Ford couldn't go wrong. Copp and Hayes agreed.

It was a staggering leap of faith, underpinned by Hayes's legendary ability to spot the right person for a job: Duckworth had never before designed a complete engine or a cylinder block, had never worked on a V8 and had never been involved with a Grand Prix engine. Cosworth had never taken on anything remotely as ambitious. But Hayes had seen Cosworth's inexorable rise through the ranks of motorsport engineering, first with its well-tuned Formula Junior engines, then with twin-cam racing engines for the Lotus-Cortinas, then the phenomenally successful SCA Formula 2 unit with its bespoke light-alloy, overhead-cam cylinder head. Hayes was convinced that Duckworth was the man for the job.

Ford's first formal acceptance of Hayes's plan came at a meeting of the Policy Committee chaired by Ford of Britain managing director Stanley Gillen towards the end of 1965. There was remarkably little fuss for a decision which was to have such far-reaching ramifications. Under the heading of 'Any Other Business', Walter Hayes merely said: 'Yes, Harley and I would like to do a Grand Prix engine.' Hayes and Copp confirmed that they had already been involved in talks with Chapman and Duckworth, and were heavily in favour. The financial outlay, although considerable in motor racing terms at the time, was a drop in Ford's ocean: as Hayes later liked to quote, the budget for the new Cosworth engines was about a tenth of the cost of adding synchromesh to the bottom gear on the Cortina gearbox.

Shortly after, Hayes was summoned to appear before the main Ford board in Dearborn to present his Grand Prix engine plan at an annual review of the company's international motorsport policy. At the head of the table sat 'Henry the Deuce' – Henry Ford II – who asked what Hayes expected the engine to achieve. 'In my opinion it will win some Grands Prix,' he said, 'and I also think that it will win a World Championship.' Eyebrows had already been raised at the cost of the project – not because anyone thought it was excessive, more because it seemed remarkably inexpensive. That, and Hayes's confidence in the plan and the people behind it, sold the project to the meeting.

Ford drafted a contract to legalise the agreement with Duckworth. It stipulated that Ford would pay £100,000 to Cosworth, and in return Cosworth and Duckworth would design and develop a pair of racing engines. The first would be a 1.6-litre Formula 2 engine, the FVA, based on the five-bearing Ford Cortina cylinder block, but fitted with a new alloy four-valve cylinder head. The other engine would be the 3.0-litre Formula 1 motor, the DFV, using cylinder heads which would be the same as those on the FVA, or developed from them. The F1 motor would be based on a new 90-degree V8 cylinder block, the design of which would only proceed once the F2 engine was proven. Both engines would wear Ford badges, rather than Cosworth ones. The F2 engine was to be developed during 1966 and Cosworth would build at least five examples for racing in 1967, while the DFV itself was to be ready to race by May that year, the date of the Monaco Grand Prix – the second round of the championship. Cosworth would build at least five DFV engines by the end of the year, and would undertake to maintain them throughout 1968. The choice of a team to

use these engines, the contract made clear, would be at Ford's discretion – although a choice had already been made…

Rumours had already been flying that Ford and Cosworth were about to do a deal, and official confirmation came from Hayes's Public Affairs department in October 1965. The contract would come into effect on 1 March 1966, at which point Ford would pay Cosworth a first instalment of £25,000 to cover initial design work on the FVA engine. A further £50,000 was to follow on 1 January 1967, and the final £25,000 a year later. Duckworth reportedly took one look at the contract, called Walter Hayes on the phone and said: 'Do you want me to read the contract, or shall I design an engine instead? I don't have time to do both.' By the beginning of 1966 Duckworth was already working on the engine, but still hadn't signed the contract, preferring to wait until the FVA design had progressed far enough for him to have confidence in the outcome. Colin Chapman was also reluctant to sign his own agreement with Ford to cover the supply of the engines for his team, because he was hoping to persuade Ford to commit itself to a longer-term deal. Walter Hayes wrote letters of intent to them both to ensure that their

Walter Hayes, with ever-present pipe, took over Ford of Britain's Public Affairs operation in 1962. Without his drive and enthusiasm the DFV would never have happened.

Henry 'the Deuce' at Le Mans in 1966. Under his 'Total Performance' ethic Ford won the Le Mans 24-hour race and dominated Formula 1.

agreement was officially recognised, pending formal signing of the full contracts.

While Duckworth turned his attention to the FVA, Lotus's 1966 F1 season got off to a surprisingly good start. The first race under the 3.0-litre Formula 1 was the non-championship South African Grand Prix, which Mike Spence won in a Lotus 25 fitted with a 2.1-litre BRM V8. At Monaco in May for the first round of the World Championship, Jim Clark took pole position in his 2.0-litre Climax-engined Lotus 33, but it was John Surtees in the V12 Ferrari who moved into an early lead. But neither Clark nor Surtees finished the race, the Ferrari succumbing to transmission problems and both works Lotuses suffering suspension failures. Jackie Stewart won in his 2.0-litre 'Tasman' BRM P261, preferred for the race over the H16 which had been tried in practice and found to struggle for gears after a few laps as the gearchange cables stretched. All this went on amid the chaos resulting from the arrival of film director John Frankenheimer and his team who were shooting the film *Grand Prix*.

At Spa, Peter Arundell's H16-engined Lotus 43 appeared, but managed only three practice laps during which he struggled to find gears before the car was

sidelined with a distributor drive failure. Several cars were eliminated in first-lap accidents in the rain, amongst them the Lotuses of Clark and Spence and the BRMs of Stewart, Hill and Bob Bondurant. Stewart came off worst, the BRM hitting a stone buttress before dropping into a ditch. He was trapped in the car for more than 10 minutes with fuel leaking all around him, before Hill and Bondurant got him free. Jochen Rindt found the weight of the Cooper-Maserati made it more stable than its rivals in the wet conditions and led most of the way, until the weather turned, and on a drying track, John Surtees could use the power of the 3.0-litre Ferrari. Surtees completed one of the best wins of his career, despite which Ferrari team manager Eugenio Dragoni was characteristically unimpressed, citing the many laps Surtees had 'allowed' a Maserati-engined car to head the Ferrari. The relationship between Surtees and Dragoni had been on the slide for some time, and matters came to a head the following week at the Le Mans 24-hour race, where Dragoni gave Surtees's opening stint to a driver he favoured, Ludovico Scarfiotti. Surtees walked out on Ferrari, a decision which probably cost him the 1966 F1 driver's title.

For the next race, the French Grand Prix at Reims early in July, Surtees appeared in the cockpit of a Maserati-engined Cooper T81. Clashing fuel contracts (Surtees to Shell, Cooper to BP) were resolved and Surtees promptly put the hefty Cooper-Maserati on the front row between his former Ferrari team-mates. Stewart was still unfit, leaving Hill as the lone BRM entry. In practice, Jim Clark was hit by a bird – a terrifying carbon copy of the scenario which had caused Alan Stacey's fatal crash at Spa six years earlier – so Pedro Rodriguez deputised, but the Lotus 33 developed an oil leak and retired. His two team-mates were already out, Spence's Lotus 25 with clutch trouble and Peter Arundell's 43 with the gear selection difficulties. It was a recurring problem for all the early H16-engined Lotus and BRM cars, caused by an inadequate cable-operated gearshift and a clutch installation which increased gearbox inertia and slowed down the gearchange.

Spirits lifted at little at Bands Hatch two weeks later, where Clark brought his 33 home in fourth place behind the two Brabham-Repcos and Graham Hill's 2.0-litre BRM. It was a similar story at Zandvoort the following week. Brabham tottered to the start line wearing a long grey beard and using walking stick, a present for his 40th birthday, but proceeded to win from Hill and Clark after an enforced pit stop robbed the Lotus of the lead.

Brabham won again at a sodden Nürburgring to set up his third World Championship, while all three works Lotuses failed. Clark raced the H16-engined Lotus 43 at power-hungry Monza, putting the car on the front row alongside the Ferraris, but retiring with transmission trouble after a poor start and a spirited fight back through the pack.

At Watkins Glen the reigning World Champion again secured a front-row position for his Lotus, but blew up his H16 engine in the process and BRM's spare engine was rapidly bolted into the back of the Lotus 43. It was a day for heavyweights: the H16 finally held together long enough to finish a race and Clark won, ahead of Rindt, Surtees and Siffert in the unfancied Cooper-Maseratis and Bruce McLaren in his McLaren M2B with its big US Ford V8. The final Grand Prix of the season, in Mexico City, saw Clark's H16 engine fail again (throwing boiling oil and water down the World Champion's neck

in the process) and more gear selection trouble in the race. Surtees won in the bulky Cooper-Maserati, while Arundell salvaged seventh for Lotus in his BRM V8-powered 33.

By their own high standards during the 1.5-litre era, it had not been a vintage season for the Lotus team. Clark was down in sixth place in the drivers' championship, and had recorded just one win during the season. Lotus-BRM had notched up 13 points, Lotus-Climax just eight. Brabham had shown the way with a new spaceframe car and a new 3.0-litre engine which was simply engineered, reliable and lightweight with just enough power to do the job. Yet for Colin Chapman and his drivers – Jim Clark would again drive for Lotus in 1967, of course, and Graham Hill would return to the team – there was cause for much optimism. Their new Cosworth engine, promising both reliability and power, was just around the corner.

GRAND PRIX RACING FORMULAS, 1906–66

Year	Main requirements	Typical car
1906	1,000kg minimum weight	7.6-litre Peugeot, 130bhp/100mph
1914	4.5-litre engine	Mercedes, 115bhp/110mph
1921	3.0-litre engine, 800kg minimum weight straight-eight,115bhp/110mph	Duesenberg
1922	2.0-litre engine	Delage V12, 190bhp/140mph
1926	1.5-litres supercharged engine, 600kg minimum weight	Bugatti Type 35
1927	1.5-litre supercharged engine, 650kg minimum weight	Delage straight-eight, 175bhp
1928	No restrictions on cars, races at least 367 miles	
1931	No restrictions on cars, races now 10 hours duration	
1932	No restrictions on cars, races now 312 miles	
1934	Maximum weight 750kg dry	Mercedes W125, 640bhp/200mph
1938	3.0-litre supercharged or 4.5-litre unsupercharged, 800kg minimum weight	Auto Union D-type, 485bhp/190mph
1945	No restrictions	
1948	1.5-litre supercharged or 4.5-litre unsupercharged	Alfa 159, 420bhp/190mph
1952	Run to F2: 750cc supercharged or 2.0-litre unsupercharged	Ferrari 500, 185bhp/150mph
1954	750cc supercharged or 2.5-litre unsupercharged	Maserati 250F, 218bhp/160mph
1961	750cc supercharged or 1.5-litre unsupercharged	Lotus 33-Climax, 213bhp/160mph
1966	1.5-litre supercharged or 3.0-litre unsupercharged	Lotus 49-Ford, 400bhp/190mph

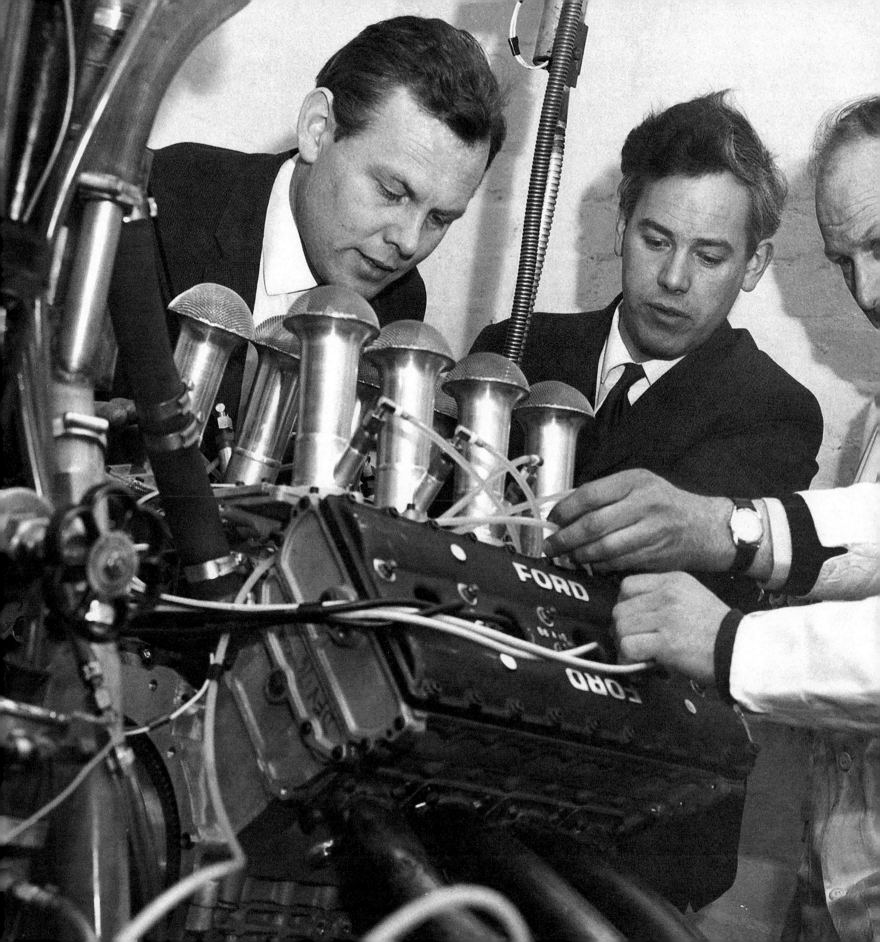

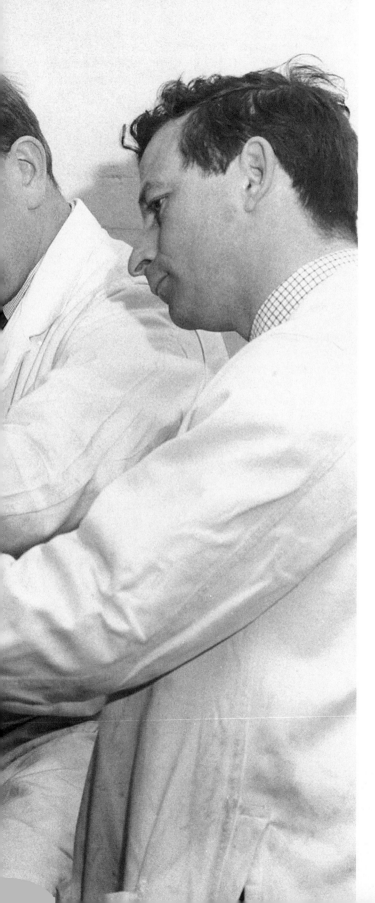

CHAPTER THREE

DESIGNING THE DFV

By the time Keith Duckworth signed his contract with Ford Motor Company to design engines for Formula 2 and Formula 1, the F2 unit was already a reality. Duckworth had begun thinking about the design of the new engine, which he called the FVA (Four Valve, series 'A') as early as July 1965 – a few months after Cosworth had completed its move from Edmonton to Northampton, but before Colin Chapman had finalised the deal with Ford to finance the project.

The new Formula 2 regulations, which were due to come into force in 1967, increased the F2 capacity limit from 1.0-litre to 1.6-litres, and rendered Cosworth's successful 997cc SCA engine obsolete. The SCA developed 115bhp on carburettors when it was first seen in 1964, and was eventually persuaded up to 140bhp or so using Lucas fuel injection, but met its match in the four-valve Honda F2 engine of 1966. By then Duckworth had recognised that the two-valve SCA was struggling for breath beyond 11,000rpm, and had turned his attention to four-valve layouts for the FVA in an effort to improve volumetric efficiency at high engine speeds.

For a given size of combustion chamber, four-valve designs can provide slightly more valve area than conventional two-valve heads and have much greater 'curtain area' – the gap between the valve and its seat all the way around the circumference of the valve head. Once the valve is lifted a long way off its seat the flow will be limited by the size and shape of the port, but while the valve is opening and closing the flow through the port will be roughly proportional to the curtain area.

Surveying the new engine on the Cosworth test bed are the four pillars of the company's success, (from left) Bill Brown, a jovial Keith Duckworth, Mike Costin and Ben Rood.

This is where four-valve systems really offer a gas-flow advantage. There are potential mechanical benefits, too, because four small valves can be lighter than two large ones, reducing valvetrain inertia. This makes it possible to increase engine speeds and thus increase the power output, without compromising reliability. The four-valve design will also have more valve seat area, which helps the exhaust valves run cooler and reduces wear.

Despite the benefits of the four-valve layout, few engines of this type had been used with any degree of success since the Second World War – though they were gradually coming back into fashion. Bentley had been a believer in four-valve engines back in the 1930s, Mercedes had used them, and the Offenhauser race engine in the US had successfully employed the same layout. The huge and rightly famous Rolls-Royce Merlin aero engine also had a four-valve combustion chamber. More recently, Borgward had built a successful four-valve F2 engine, and Coventry Climax had introduced a four-valve version of the FWMV V8 in 1965. BRM was working on four-valve heads for the fearsomely complex H16, and would later use them for its 3.0-litre V12, while Ferrari was also looking at four-valve layouts for its V12s.

Duckworth hoped that with four valves per cylinder the FVA would breathe better at high revs than the SCA had done, and at the same time he aimed to introduce some circumferential swirl, a bulk movement of the air/fuel charge in the cylinder around the cylinder axis. Swirl helped to fully mix the air and fuel in the combustion chamber, and set up turbulence in the mixture which promoted rapid and efficient burning of the charge. The SCA had always run best with lots of ignition advance – up to 49 degrees – indicating that combustion was too slow, and despite all kinds of development work on port layouts and combustion chamber shapes the problem never disappeared.

Duckworth quickly dismissed the 'classic' hemispherical combustion chamber as outdated and inefficient. In its original form, with two opposed valves, a central spark plug and a flat-topped piston running in an engine with a relatively low compression ratio, the hemispherical chamber was an attractive layout. The dome-shape combustion chamber could accommodate large valves to raise volumetric efficiency, the ports could easily be aimed upwards at a convenient angle and the uncomplicated combustion chamber shape with the plug in the centre promoted complete combustion.

Four-valve engines were out of fashion early in the 1960s, but back in the '30s W. O. Bentley had been a big believer in their benefits. This is the 1930 Le Mans-winning car with drivers Glen Kidston and Woolf Barnato.

Keith Duckworth (left) and Harley Copp examine Cosworth's 1.6-litre Formula 2 engine, the FVA, based on a production Ford Cortina block.

But as engine speeds rose and fuel quality improved, the limitations of the hemispherical chamber became apparent. The volume of the combustion chamber was large, which meant it took a long time for the flame front, starting at the central spark plug, to burn through the mixture. Ignition advance in the region of 50 degrees was not uncommon on engines with hemispherical combustion chambers.

Meanwhile, the large surface area of the chamber provided an effective path for heat loss, reducing the engine's thermal efficiency. On top of that, the large chamber limited the compression ratio. Higher-quality fuels were becoming available which were more resistant to knock, and that meant higher compression

ratios could be employed without risk to the engine, and higher efficiency could be obtained. With a hemispherical combustion chamber shape, the only way engine designers could reduce the volume above the piston at top dead centre, and so raise the compression ratio, was to fit domed pistons. These heavier pistons resulted in an increase in the reciprocating mass of the engine which tended to keep engine speeds down.

Perhaps more importantly, during combustion, the combustion chamber was no longer a neat hemisphere, but instead was more the shape of half a coconut – or what Keith Duckworth was often heard to describe as an 'orange peel shape'. This thin shell-like volume was bounded by the hemispherical shape of the chamber

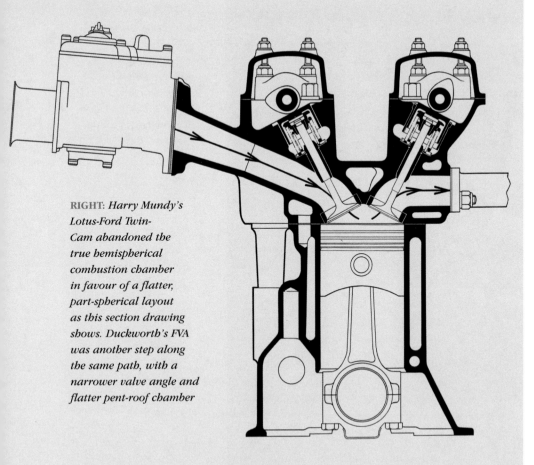

RIGHT: *Harry Mundy's Lotus-Ford Twin-Cam abandoned the true hemispherical combustion chamber in favour of a flatter, part-spherical layout as this section drawing shows. Duckworth's FVA was another step along the same path, with a narrower valve angle and flatter pent-roof chamber*

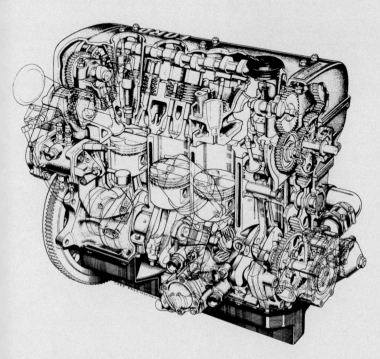

LEFT: *The cutaway drawing of the FVA Formula 2 engine shows the pent-roof combustion chamber with four valves, and a narrow included angle between them. The basic head layout was carried over to the DFV, although there were detail differences.*

in the head above, and the domed crown of the piston underneath. The flame front somehow had to fight its way down to the lowest recesses of this shape to burn all the air/fuel mixture, and some designers found two or even three spark plugs were necessary for reliable and complete combustion.

A better solution was to move from a strict 'hemispherical' shape to one which is more correctly termed a 'part-hemispherical', in that it is less than exactly half a sphere. The Lotus Twin-Cam head, designed by Harry Mundy in 1963, is one example. By reducing the angle between the valve stems from the conventional 90 degrees to 54 degrees, Mundy brought the valves into a more vertical position and flattened out the combustion chamber. This reduced the volume above the piston at top dead centre, and reduced the area contributing to heat loss from the combustion chamber. A convenient benefit was that the physical size of the cylinder head was reduced because the camshafts were brought closer together by the narrower included angle between the valves.

For the FVA, Duckworth chose to abandon the hemispherical/part-spherical head and instead opt for a 'pent-roof' design, with two pairs of parallel valves at an included angle of just 40 degrees. This ensured a compact combustion chamber, which could be used with a light, flat-top piston and still generate a compression ratio around 10:1. With four large valves the pent-roof design was almost inevitable anyway, unless the designer was prepared to abandon neat parallel pairs of valves, and instead, splay out the valve stems so that the valve heads formed something approximating a part-sphere. Ludwig Apfelbeck's Formula 2 engine for BMW used just such a 'radial valve' layout, and amply demonstrated one of the main drawbacks: valve stems emerged at all sorts of odd angles, so the valve gear was complex. Jack Brabham called it the 'high and heavy' engine, with some justification. In the case of the Apfelbeck engine, the complicated valve gear proved unable to cope with the rigours of racing at 10,000rpm, and after much development BMW dropped the idea.

The simplest arrangement of the valves had them laid out in pairs – two inlets on one side and two exhausts on the other – but for a while, Duckworth played around with a diagonally-opposed layout with an inlet and an exhaust valve on each side of the chamber. The idea was that the air/fuel mixture would be entering the combustion chamber almost tangentially, and this would encourage the mixture to swirl around the cylinder axis.

Duckworth rejected the 'radial' valve layout because of complications with the manifolding and valve gear. At BMW, Ludwig Apfelbeck designed this radial-valve four, but it proved to be heavy and unreliable.

The result would be better mixing of fuel with the intake air and more rapid propagation of the flame, improving combustion. Duckworth got as far as producing detail drawings for this diagonally-opposed layout before he realised that the circumferential swirl it produced – something he had striven for on the SCA engine – had almost no beneficial effect because the spark plug was in the middle of the combustion chamber, where gas was hardly moving at all. The tangential swirl only benefited an engine with an off-centre spark plug location, like the SCA.

Duckworth concluded that the only way to utilise the movement of the mixture generated by the diagonally-opposed four-valve layout was to add two extra spark plugs off-centre, but he rejected that idea as 'silly'. BMW didn't think so: their replacement for the Apfelbeck in 1968 was the 'Diametral', with diagonally-opposed valves and three spark plugs per cylinder. It won races, but eventually BMW tried a conventional paired-valve layout which produced virtually the same power output with a much better torque curve. By then, the FVA had won a lot of races – including all the Formula 2 races in 1967 – using just such a layout. If nothing else, pairing the valves at least made the plumbing of the inlet and exhaust manifolds simpler as there needed to be just one of each. By contrast, the diagonally-opposed layout required an inlet and an exhaust manifold on each side of the head – bad enough on an in-line four like the FVA, but when the engine was doubled up into a V8 as was planned, the plumbing would have been a nightmare.

But Duckworth did not give up on swirl, and the efficient combustion it generates. Instead, he designed the valves and ports of the FVA to generate swirl in a different direction, around an axis perpendicular to the cylinder axis and parallel to the gudgeon pin. This ensured that the air/fuel mixture was well mixed and directed the charge towards the central spark plug.

The FVA's alloy cylinder head topped off a production Ford Cortina block, which now carried a geartrain at the front end to drive a pair of overhead camshafts. The valves had double valve springs and were operated through bucket tappets. Duckworth retained the original Ford camshaft, low down on the right-hand side of the block, to drive the distributor and oil pump. Unusually, the cams were covered by a single cast aluminium cam cover rather than two separate covers, made possible because of the narrow valve angle and close-set camshafts. In this form the engine ran on the test bed at

Northampton in February 1966, and it quickly delivered the 200bhp output which Duckworth felt would make it competitive in Formula 2 – and which would make the doubled-up F1 V8 viable. That summer, Mike Costin had begun track tests with a Brabham F2 car fitted with an FVB engine, a short-stroke 1,498cc version of the FVA which more closely represented one bank of the DFV that was to follow. Costin also ran the car in club races, where it recorded a number of wins and lap records.

Testing proved that while Duckworth's head design was sound the narrow-angle valve layout did not go far enough. The engine would tolerate higher compression, which meant that the combustion chamber had to be even smaller. Domed pistons solved the problem, but a better solution would have been to reduce the included angle between the valve stems, flattening out the roof of the combustion chamber so that the volume decreased even further. The DFV would follow that route.

With the FVA up and running, Duckworth's attention turned to the DFV early in 1966. The V8 would be a much more exacting project, as it was much more than just a new cylinder head and a gear-drive for the camshafts. For the DFV, Duckworth would have to design a brand-new block, drawing on Cosworth's experience of modifying production cylinder blocks for use in racing. It was this experience, Duckworth believed, which was far more useful than any attempts to calculate the stresses in the engine – such a complex process that it would almost inevitably be subject to assumption and error.

In addition to laying out a block suitable for a 400bhp V8, Duckworth had the additional task of ensuring that it met the requirements of Colin Chapman and his designer Maurice Philippe in its role as a stressed part of

DESIGNED FOR THE DFV: THE LOTUS 49

While Cosworth had completed work on the engine, Lotus had been building a new car to take it. The design was deliberately kept simple so that it would give little trouble while Team Lotus sorted out its new engine. Maurice Philippe schemed an aluminium alloy monocoque, much the same in concept to the BRM-engined Type 43, which ended in a 360-degree stressed section behind the driver's shoulders. The only 'bodywork' was the detachable glassfibre nose-cone. Bag tanks carrying 15 gallons of fuel were housed in the sides of the monocoque, feeding through non-return valves to a 10-gallon tank behind the driver's seat from which the engine drew its supply. Under acceleration fuel surged backwards, keeping the centre tank full.

The suspension followed Type 43 practice with inboard coil/damper units at the front operated by top rocker arms, and a pair of lower links locating a cast upright which carried the stub axle and internally ventilated brake disc. The rear suspension was by single top links which picked up on the back of the DFV cylinder heads, a lower wishbone mounted on the final drive unit and twin radius rods which fed their loads into the side of the monocoque.

The 49 won four races in 1967, four more in Graham Hill's championship year of 1968, two in 1969 and one more in 1970. As late as August 1970, months after the debut of the 72, Team Lotus new-boy Emerson Fittipaldi brought his 49C home fourth at the Nürburgring, and privateers ran 49s well into 1971. It served its purpose brilliantly.

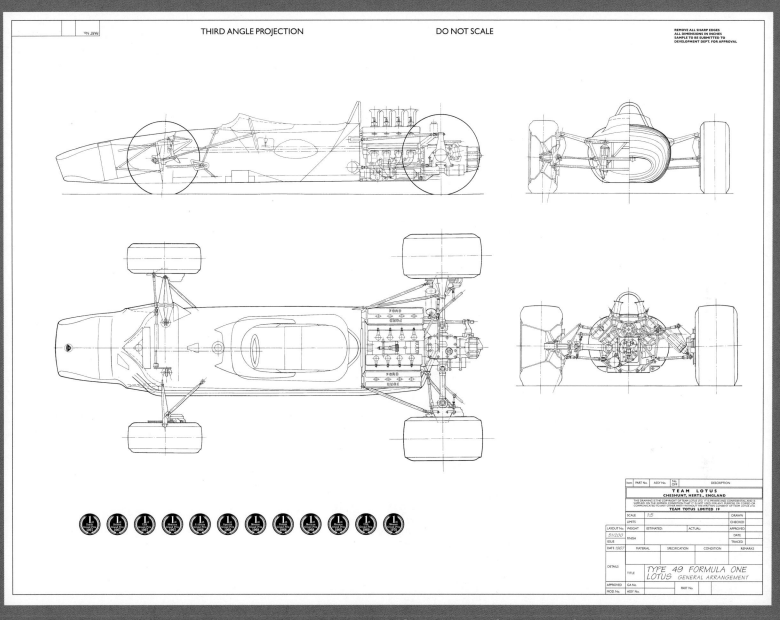

Item	PART No.	ASSY No.	No. OFF		DESCRIPTION		

TEAM LOTUS
CHESHUNT, HERTS., ENGLAND

THIS DRAWING IS THE COPYRIGHT OF TEAM LOTUS LTD. IT IS PRIVATE AND CONFIDENTIAL AND IS SUPPLIED ON THE EXPRESS CONDITION THAT IT IS NOT USED FOR ANY PURPOSE OR COPIED OR COMMUNICATED TO ANY OTHER PARTY WITHOUT THE WRITTEN CONSENT OF TEAM LOTUS LTD.

TEAM LOTUS LIMITED 19

SCALE	1:5			DRAWN	
LIMITS				CHECKED	
LAYOUT No.	WEIGHT	ESTIMATED:	ACTUAL:	APPROVED	
51/200				DATE	
ISSUE	FINISH			TRACED	
DATE 1967	MATERIAL	SPECIFICATION	CONDITION	REMARKS	

DETAILS

TITLE TYPE 49 FORMULA ONE
LOTUS GENERAL ARRANGEMENT

APPROVED	GA No.		PART No.	
MOD. No.	ASSY No.			

The Lotus 49 general arrangement drawing. Note the ZF gearbox at the back of the car with its input shaft slung under the rear axle line, the tidy engine installation with the profile of the cam covers matching the cross-section of the monocoque, and the compactness of the car as a whole. The 49 was deliberately kept simple, so Team Lotus could concentrate on sorting the engine. Today, copies of these drawings are available from www.classicteamlotus.co.uk.

the car's chassis – just as the BRM H16 engine was doing in the 1966 Lotus and BRM Formula 1 cars. Not that the stresses involved were a major headache because, as Duckworth would later point out, the internal loads in an engine were considerably greater than anything that would be imposed on it by the suspension mountings. To simplify the engine installation in the car, Duckworth quickly decided that the front face of the engine would be flat, so it would mate neatly with the monocoque. The cylinder heads, cam covers, gearbox mountings and the lower crankcase casting would all have to be designed in such a way that they could carry loads from the rear suspension into the car's monocoque.

The design process for the DFV would also be different to the FVA because Duckworth would no longer be restricted by the use of the production block. So, instead of accepting fixed cylinder bore spacing and head bolt locations, for instance, Duckworth now had the freedom to specify them as he saw fit. Several weeks passed while he thought hard about the general layout of the new engine, but only one major decision was taken, and one drawing produced. The dimensions of the rear face of the engine had to be decided so that the German ZF company could begin work on the car's

Early DFV crankshaft, pistons, connecting rods and cylinder liners. Note the single-plane crank configuration, with all the bearing journals lying in the same plane: the firing order resulting from this layout simplified exhaust system design, but led to problems with vibration later.

final drive and gearbox. As a result, Duckworth's first DFV drawing showed the layout of the flywheel housing and the mounting for the starter, which he had decided to accommodate at the gearbox housing rather than in the conventional position alongside the engine. Other Formula 1 teams were now using Hewland gearboxes with their easy-to-change ratios, but Chapman was never a fan of the Hewland. Instead, he preferred to stick with ZF, who had supplied transaxles for the Lotus 25/33 cars, and had also built the transmissions for Lotus Indy cars and Ford's GT40s, which would win Le Mans that year.

The rest of the engine took some time to scheme out. The very freedom which was allowing Duckworth to design whatever he wanted was also slowing down the process of deciding how best to lay out the engine, because there was no fixed starting point. Whenever Duckworth encountered a problem in one area, another area could be modified to suit, which in turn meant modifications might be necessary somewhere else. One of the key decisions was the location of the cylinder head bolts, and after several weeks of deep thinking, but little visible progress, Mike Costin felt it necessary to 'read the riot act'.

With a decision made about the position of the head bolts, the rest of the engine began to take shape. Duckworth mostly worked at home to avoid the distractions of his office at Cosworth, where he was managing director as well as chief engine designer. Every week or so he would meet with Mike Costin and design engineer Mike Hall, who was working on the detail designs of the engine's ancillaries. Duckworth also spent some time at Ford's research and development centre at Dunton in Essex, talking to Harley Copp and other Ford engineers, and using Ford's metallurgical facilities. But most of the time Duckworth was at his drawing board, often for up to 16 hours a day, for a period of around nine months. Famously, he said his diet consisted mostly of steak and cabbage, and as a result he lost 40lb.

Central to the design of the new engine was Duckworth's first-ever cylinder block design. With two banks of four cylinders, primary engine balance could be achieved either with 90 or 180 degrees between the banks – the latter producing a flat-eight which would be too wide to comfortably marry up to a slim Formula 1 chassis. So the choice of a 90-degree V8 was almost inevitable. Duckworth was keen to make the block as short as possible, to aid the 'packaging' of the main elements in the car. Fuel was best carried somewhere near the centre of gravity of the car so that the varying

Front end of the DFV, showing the triangular layout of the belt-drive for the oil and water pumps. The toothed wheel fitted to the nose of the crankshaft provides a trigger signal for the ignition system.

load during the race made as little difference to the weight distribution, and therefore to the car's handling, as possible. The suspension set-up could then be more nearly optimised, instead of being a compromise between full-tank and empty-tank running.

A long engine lengthens the car's wheelbase leading to sluggish handling, or forces the designer to provide extra fuel capacity by bulging the tank sideways, increasing frontal area and reducing the car's top speed. The DFV turned out to be wider than it is long, 27in (686mm) wide and only 21.45in (545mm) long, the width between the cam covers conveniently matching the proposed width of the Lotus 49 monocoque. Duckworth came up with a mounting system which fed

loads through plates into the cam carriers at the top and through two bolts into the corners of the lower crankcase/sump casting at the base of the engine. The lower mounting bolts had to be 9in (229mm) apart to match the narrow base of the Lotus monocoque – a dimension which had been scientifically derived from the width of Jim Clark's bottom!

The block and the top half of the crankcase formed a single, asymmetrical casting in aluminium alloy, which extended down to the crankshaft centreline. A horizontal web between the two banks of cylinders stiffened the whole engine. 'Wet' cast-iron cylinder liners were pressed into place, located at the top by flanges and sealed at the bottom by O-rings. The

bore of 3.375in (85.73mm) was the same as the FVA engine, and the stroke had been shortened from 2.72in (69.09mm) to 2.55in (64.77mm) to bring the capacity within the 3.0-litre limit, at 2,993cc. As had become the norm for high-speed racing engines, the DFV was significantly oversquare, the short stroke keeping the maximum piston speed down to a relatively low 3,825 feet (1,166m) per minute at the initial 9,000rpm rev limit. The left-hand bank of cylinders was 0.4in (9.5mm) further forward than the right-hand bank so that conventional connecting rods and side-by-side big end bearings could be used, instead of the complex, and heavy, forked conrods which would have been necessary if the block had been symmetrical. The rods were forged steel with conventional big-end bearings split across their diameter at 90 degrees to the rod shank.

The long connecting rods, with a 4.1:1 ratio of rod length to crank throw, minimised out-of-balance forces and piston accelerations. By reducing the side-thrust of the pistons on the cylinder walls they also reduced power-sapping internal friction – although using such long rods did mean the engine had to be slightly wider. Duckworth specified smooth internal surfaces within the crankcase which improved the internal aerodynamics of the block and further reduced mechanical losses. Following Cosworth's experience with the FVA, the compression ratio was raised to around 11:1. The pistons were light alloy forgings by Hepworth & Grandage (Cosworth did not yet have its own foundry) with solid skirts and flat tops, provided with small valve cutaways in the crowns for clearance. There were three piston rings – a narrow Dykes top ring, a compression ring, and an oil control ring.

Duckworth had the choice of two crankshaft configurations, single-plane and two-plane, and opted for the single-plane crank. The two-plane or cruciform crankshaft, as used on almost all road-going V8s, can be arranged to provide perfect secondary balance, which is what makes most V8-engined cars so smooth. Firing intervals are regular across the engine as a whole, but irregular along each bank of cylinders. This gives the engine its characteristic V8 burble, but makes it difficult to arrange an efficient exhaust system, and as Coventry Climax found out, exhaust primaries on one bank need to be connected to the other. The crankshaft itself is also heavy. A flat or single-plane crank, by contrast, makes exhaust tuning easy because it gives the engine even firing intervals on each bank, and effectively turns the V8 into two in-line fours sharing a common crankshaft.

Each cylinder bank can be given its own simple and compact four-cylinder-type exhaust manifold which is light and easy to tune for optimum cylinder scavenging, and of a type with which Cosworth was already very familiar. The downside is that a V8 with a single-plane crankshaft still has some secondary out-of-balance forces which cause the whole engine to vibrate at twice the frequency of crankshaft rotation, but Duckworth accepted that as a reasonable trade-off for the simpler exhaust system. With cylinders numbered 1 to 4 from the front of the right-hand bank, and 5 to 8 from the front of the left-hand back, the firing order worked out as 1-8-3-6-4-5-2-7. The DFV crankshaft had five main bearings, the same size as those on the FVA. There were four crank-pins, each one hollow (to save weight) and carrying two connecting rods as was usual V8 practice. The crankshaft was a nitrided, fully machined, steel forging carried in steel-backed lead indium bearings and weighing 32lb (14.5kg).

At the back the crankshaft carried an eight-bolt flange and a 9.7in-diameter flywheel, into which the starter gear teeth were machined. A 7.25in clutch was specified, a Borg & Beck twin-plate diaphragm-spring design using sintered clutch plates which were more resistant to heat than a conventional lined plate, although sharper in operation. Provision was made for a torsional vibration damper on the nose of the crankshaft, but Duckworth did not expect it to be necessary during 1967, when Cosworth hoped to restrict the engine speed to 9,000rpm – though it was expected that ultimately, experience with the engine would allow a safe rev-limit of up to 11,500rpm.

Two-stage gearing from the nose of the crankshaft drove a half-speed shaft located between the two banks of cylinders, and from this a pair of gears right in the centre of the engine drove a horizontal auxiliaries shaft high up in the 'V' of the engine. The rear of this drove the alternator and the distributor for the Lucas Lutronic transistorised ignition system, while the front drove the metering unit for the Lucas Mk1 fuel injection.

The second job of the half-speed shaft was to drive the geartrains for the camshafts, which had been deliberately designed with a considerable flywheel effect to damp out torsional vibrations within the valvetrain. Finally, the half-speed shaft drove a cogged belt drive at the front of the engine which powered two accessory shafts, one on each side of the sump. On the left-hand side the accessory shaft drove a water pump for the left-hand cylinder bank, the oil pressure pump, and

Right-hand side of the DFV shows how the water and oil-scavenge pumps were low down on the side of the engine. In the late 1970s the pump installation was tidied up to maximise the space available for 'ground-effect' venturi tunnels either side of the engine.

Theo Page's cutaway of the DFV, issued by Ford at the engine's unveiling in 1967. The complex geartrain near the front of the engine drives the camshafts, injection metering unit, distributor, alternator and the belt drive for the oil and water pumps.

a mechanical fuel pump, while the right-hand shaft powered the water pump for the right-hand bank and two eccentric-rotor scavenge pumps for the dry-sump system. The layout of the pumps and accessories had been broadly defined by Keith Duckworth, but the detail arrangement was the work of Mike Hall, ex-BRM, who would later design the BD and GA engines for Cosworth.

The bottom of the sump was just 5.23in (133mm) from the centreline of the crankshaft, giving the DFV a very low centre of gravity and allowing reasonable ground clearance despite the intention of running the output shaft from the clutch under the final drive to a rear-mounted gearbox. The low centre of gravity would also contribute to the car's handling and

roadholding. The sump was a complex light-alloy casting incorporating the lower main bearing caps, each held in place by two through bolts, and the internal surfaces were curved to minimise oil churning losses. The sump was split into front and rear sections at the number three main bearing, and each section was provided with its own scavenge pump, driven off the right-hand accessory shaft. Tubular sections along the side of the crankcase/sump casting and across the front (the latter carrying coolant to the left-hand water pump) served to stiffen the casting, improving its ability to resist loads being fed from the suspension to the lower engine mounting bolts.

At the top of the engine, the DFV carried cylinder

heads which were similar to, but subtly different from, the head that Keith Duckworth had designed for the FVA. The DFV used two identical light alloy head castings, with pressed-in valve seat inserts and valve guides. The inlet valves were slightly larger than the exhaust valves, 1.32in diameter compared to 1.14in. The ports were almost straight to allow maximum gas flow, the inlet ports being slightly longer than the exhausts. In both cases the ports serving a pair of valves were blended together inside the head, and emerged as a single port at the manifold. Duckworth had tightened up the valve angle still further from the FVA, each pair of valves now being 16 degrees from the cylinder centreline instead of 20 degrees.

Each head was retained by ten studs in threaded holes in the cylinder block and eight bolts which picked up on flanges on the block casting. These provided a ring of six fixings around each cylinder bore, which helped to clamp the heads to the cylinder block forcefully enough to resist the distorting loads imposed by the engine mountings at the front of the power unit and the suspension mountings through the cylinder heads and gearbox final drive casing at the rear. To ensure that the grip between heads and block was sufficient to deal with the chassis loads and to resist combustion forces, the heads were assembled without any form of head gasket – although coolant passages were provided with recesses at the joint face for O-rings. The heads were installed so that the inlet ports on each cylinder bank faced inwards, and the exhausts faced out. This left plenty of space for the exhaust manifolds alongside the engine, leaving the 'V' for the fuel injection metering unit, the ignition distributor and tuned-length intake ram pipes which fed through slide throttles. The low overall height of the engine allowed the long intake pipes to sit neatly behind the driver's headrest.

Cast light-alloy cam carriers were fitted above the heads, each carrying a pair of chilled-iron camshafts running in steel-backed bearings and incorporating 16 guide bores for the bucket tappets operating the valves. As on the FVA, a single, shallow cast alloy cam cover enclosed the valvegear on each cylinder head. On the DFV these also provided the top engine mounting on each side, the stresses being fed into the engine through a reinforcing tube along the length of the cam-carrier casting. This stiffened the casting, and avoided any problems with tappets seizing due to flexing of the cam-carrier. Four holes in the tube provided access to the

10mm spark plugs, which Ford insisted were of the in-house Autolite brand.

The first DFV was completed in April 1967, but early tests on the dynamometer were not as trouble-free as Keith Duckworth and his colleagues would have hoped. The oil drains from the cylinder head were too small, and at high revs oil was collecting in the cylinder heads and emerging from the breathers instead of draining back to the sump where the scavenge pumps could collect it. Costin and Duckworth tried several 'lash-up' solutions and eventually sorted out the internal breathing, but early engines had to be fitted with big external breathing tubes connected to tin boxes on the right-hand cam cover. The reward for the hard-working Cosworth team was a power run where the DFV recorded a peak figure of 408bhp, comfortably exceeding Duckworth's initial target of 400bhp.

Another early problem was with the geartrain driving the camshafts. During one of the dynamometer runs one of the timing gears lost a tooth, though by that time the engine had done a lot of test running so the Cosworth team felt the service life of the gears was acceptable. It turned out to be a problem however, which nearly robbed the DFV of its first Grand Prix win, and would

April 1967 and the DFV is piped-up on the dynamometer and ready to run, and Keith Duckworth checks over his masterpiece.

become an ever bigger issue as the engine's early career progressed.

The DFV was officially presented to the motor sport press on 25 April 1967, at Ford Motor Company's offices in Regent Street, London. The example on display was not quite the pristine showpiece that might have been expected for such a launch: the scuffs and scratches on the cam covers showed this was the real thing, and it had already been involved in early tests. Colin Chapman and Graham Hill were in attendance, along with Sir Patrick Hennessy and Harley Copp from Ford, together with invited motoring correspondents and members of the specialist motorsport press. Ford's Public Affairs chief Walter Hayes was the host. Some time earlier Hayes had mentioned to Denis Holmes of the *Daily Mail* that the new engine would be a V8, but Holmes was one of the few who knew that Cosworth and Ford would not be following the trend towards complex, multi-cylinder engines which by now seemed unstoppable.

Ferrari and Honda already had V12s, Weslake had a V12 on the drawing board, and BRM were working on V12s and H16s. V12s seemed the minimum required to compete, and there were fanciful ideas that F1 might soon see 24-cylinder engines competing. The theory was that smaller, lighter pistons reduced internal stresses, but Duckworth felt that piston acceleration was more important – and that frictional losses in multi-cylinder engines counted against them. Even so, Hayes realised that a V8 was going to seem old-fashioned, if not outdated and he recalled later that when the DFV V8 was unveiled there was a shocked silence, followed by a few giggles. Those who laughed would come to regret it soon enough.

Hayes's speech introducing the DFV began by explaining why Ford had got involved with Formula 1. 'We decided to begin this racing engine programme in November 1965. There were several substantial reasons which made it look like a good idea. There was the question of national prestige, which may sound a little presumptuous, but is nevertheless nothing but the truth. If you care to look at the history of motorsport as it has developed this century in Europe, you will find that, year after year, the Italians were dominant. It was not until 1959 that Jack Brabham won the World Championship for Britain in a Cooper and since that historical date, British cars or drivers have remained unchallenged.' Tony Vandervell would no doubt argue that the British 'arrived' in Grand Prix racing somewhat earlier, when the Vanwalls won the Constructors' Cup in 1958…

'Motorsport has become the one form of international sport in which Britain's pre-eminence has been undisputed,' Hayes went on, 'for one World Football Cup doesn't make more than a summer. Year after year British saloons and sports cars have swept to triumphant victories in races and rallies the world over… At the end of 1965 Coventry Climax said they would make no more Grand Prix engines. And Honda was coming in with more and more might and money. Ferrari was still fighting for supremacy… The British constructors – men like Chapman and McLaren and Brabham and Broadley – who lacked the capital and resources, were, naturally enough, worried about their competitive prospects. There was even some talk of an approach to the Government to seek assistance for the development of a British racing engine. There were people who pointed out that British prestige in international motor sport was an important, if indefinable, component of the growing success of the British production car in export markets.'

Hayes went on to give examples of Ford engines developed for competition, and showed how the competition lessons returned to the road in cars like the Lotus-Cortina. He also explained the thinking behind a V8 engine, and with his Public Affairs remit firmly in mind he tried to plant a link in the assembled media-men's minds between the new racing engine and Ford's more mundane road cars. 'BRM had a 16-cylinder engine in development and we knew that the Honda would produce between 420bhp and 440bhp. The brilliant Harry Weslake was working with Dan Gurney on a unit of his own design. If we could aim for a V8 which would be, in a sense, two Cortina-based Formula 2 engines in V configuration, we could perhaps expect 400bhp. Would that be enough?

'There were other things we could have done, but at the back of all our minds at that time was the knowledge that the overwhelming importance of the programme was the ability to learn from racing and then apply that knowledge to mutual customers. Ford was in the V-engine business in a big way from Corsair to Zodiac and this was of material importance,' said Hayes. Diplomatically he omitted to mention that the V-engines in question were cast-iron, two-valve pushrod V4s and V6s which had practically nothing in common with Duckworth's masterpiece.

'Colin Chapman agreed to design a completely new racing car,' Hayes went on, using understandable PR man's license to distort the order of events, 'of which the keynote would be lightness and simplicity… This

*The press launch
for the DFV engine,
at Ford's Regent
Street headquarters.
Graham Hill surveys
the engine he would
soon be helping to
develop in the Lotus
49 – and which would
let him down on its
first appearance in a
Grand Prix...*

was clearly a key decision because it then enabled us to go ahead with the design of a car and an engine together – two components of the whole made for each other. That is why the new Ford Formula 1 engine will only go in the new Lotus chassis. It was designed that way.'

Hayes ended by downplaying the DFV's potential, warning that some teething problems were almost inevitable. 'As I speak I have no way of knowing the outcome. I have no doubt that there are races we are not going to finish – problems we are going to discover, faces that will occasionally look a little red. In racing it was ever thus. But I have no doubt either that when you are buying a family Ford in the '70s a lot of the aches and

pains we are about to endure will be a source of your pride and contentment as an owner – even if you have no desire to exceed 40mph.'

Surprisingly, neither of Britain's motorsport weeklies were moved to comment in any detail on the new engine being a 'mere' V8. *Motoring News*, the motor sport newspaper, carried a Theo Page cutaway drawing of the new engine on the front page of its 27 April edition. 'On Tuesday Ford sprang a surprise on the British Press by unveiling their new V8 3-litre Formula 1 engine which has been designed and built by Cosworth,' said the brief front-page story, 'This 400bhp engine will be used exclusively by Lotus and will probably make its debut in the Dutch Grand Prix at Zandvoort'. Inside, two whole pages were devoted to the new engine, including the text of Walter Hayes's speech and a technical description of the engine supplied by Ford and written by Joe Lowry. 'The new 3-litre Formula 1 engine from Ford is undoubtedly one of the biggest motor racing stories in recent times, which is why we are devoting two pages to it,' said the introduction. The single photograph showed a DFV on a dynamometer, with Bill Brown, Ben Rood, Mike Costin and a troubled-looking Keith Duckworth in attendance.

The following day *Autosport*, the other British motorsport weekly, also reported on the DFV unveiling. 'The announcement this week of the Cosworth-designed and developed Ford Formula One engine must be a cause of some concern for Lotus' rivals in the Grand Epreuve field,' said *Autosport*'s editorial column, penned no doubt by Gregor Grant. 'With minimum weight, 400bhp and Jim Clark and Graham Hill as their drivers, Team Lotus and Ford must be very strong contenders for World Championship victory once they have got their new car sorted out.' Like *Motoring News*, *Autosport* led its brief news story on the unveiling with the cutaway drawing, but left its own in-depth description of the DFV until the following week, and was unable to resist using the cutaway drawing again to head the feature.

Assistant editor Patrick McNally's story, accompanied by detail photographs of the engine, concentrated on the technical features, and concluded by predicting great things. 'With its characteristics of light weight, compactness and comparative simplicity, the Ford F1 engine should be a real force to be reckoned with in this year's Grandes Epreuves.'

Much later, Walter Hassan would give his verdict on the design of the DFV in his book *Climax in Coventry*. 'In many ways the DFV was a logical development of the work we had carried out at Coventry Climax,' said Hassan. 'The four-valve layout was broadly the same, though the included valve angles were reduced to 32 degrees; our racing experience indicated that we should continue to reduce the included angles – the FPF angle was 66 degrees, the FWMV V-8 was 60 degrees (two-valve and four-valve), and the unraced flat-16 FWMW was 48 degrees – and any engine we might have raced after the flat-16 would certainly have approached Cosworth's figure.' Another area of similarity, Hassan said, was the use of a flat-plane crankshaft, and the relatively simple exhaust manifolding which it allowed. 'I notice that Keith's engine was designed with a flat-crank from the word "go", which eliminated any of the exhaust-system conundrums we had had to solve a few years earlier.'

Walter Hayes tried to draw parallels between the DFV V8 and the V-engines in Ford's contemporary European road car range – but the 'Essex' V6 in this MkIV Zodiac had almost nothing in common with Cosworth's masterpiece.

CHAPTER FOUR

TRIUMPH AND TRAGEDY: 1967–68

As the 1966 season drew to a close, Henry Taylor, Ford's competitions manager, approached BRM team leader Graham Hill. Had Hill ever considered a return to his old team, Lotus? Although Hill had won the 1962 World Championship with BRM, the 1966 season had been disappointing. The 2.0-litre V8 BRMs were nimble, but couldn't catch the Ferraris or the Brabhams on a fast circuit, while the new H16 was heavy and was proving capable of catastrophic failures in an extraordinary range of different modes. Colin Chapman had apparently told Taylor that Hill was a fixture at BRM, but Hill was starting to think that he was so much a part of the furniture that his influence on the team's direction was waning. A change must have seemed like an attractive idea.

'Obviously Ford wanted to safeguard their £10,000 [sic] investment in a Ford engine so they had to have two drivers,' said Hill in his autobiography, *Life at the Limit*, written in 1969. 'If Jimmy Clark caught a cold, or something stupid like that, or had an accident, or if the cars kept breaking down, the Championship could be lost. So they wanted a second string to their bow. Also, if they had two top-rank drivers, obviously no other team could have them and this would reduce their opposition – so it had a two-fold benefit.'

Clark's green and yellow Lotus has just lapped Ludovico Scarfiotti's scarlet Ferrari, which is heading for sixth place. This shot gives a good view of the air deflector windscreen which generated a jet of air to deflect rain drops and debris away from the driver's face.

Hill discussed the move with BRM, and considered staying if certain changes were made to the way the team operated, but eventually decided to join Lotus. 'At the time I thought it was a hell of a gamble,' he wrote. 'I was stepping out of a number one position with a team which I had been with for several years straight into what had been the enemy camp, where they already had an established number one, who'd been there for several years and who, quite rightly, would expect to be given preferential treatment.' That number one, of course, was Jim Clark. Hill moved to Lotus as joint number one, though he must have known the close working relationship between Clark and Chapman (and perhaps a hint of bitterness over Hill's departure from Lotus years earlier) would always leave him at a slight disadvantage. But the arrangement worked out well, and the two drivers 'got on famously'.

It was Walter Hayes who had been behind the plan. As Eric Dymock explained in his revealing portrait, *Jim Clark* (Dove Publishing 1997) Hayes lured Hill away from BRM with a £10,000 retainer, twice what Clark had been getting from Lotus. Ford contributed a further £5,000 to raise Clark's remuneration to the same level, and put in place a bonus scheme for points

ABOVE: *Graham Hill joined Jim Clark at Team Lotus in 1967, after seven successful seasons with BRM.*

RIGHT: *Early DFV crankshafts were machined from a steel billet, but once serious production of the engines got underway a Nitrided, forged-steel item was used. A faulty batch in 1970 severely hampered the production of engines.*

finishes, from £1,500 for a win down to £100 for sixth place. In 1967 they were considerable sums of money: £1,500 would have been more than the average Briton's annual earnings, and £10,000 would have bought two comfortable houses.

Ironically, Hill's first race for Lotus, the South African Grand Prix in January 1967, reunited him with the BRM H16. This time it was in the back of a Lotus 43 – the same chassis, 43/1, that Clark had used to win at Watkins Glen the previous October. Problems in practice left Hill well down the grid, and in the race he put a wheel up on one of Kyalami's sloping kerbs and bent a wishbone. That lowered the ride-height on one side, and caused an oil pipe under the car to wear on the road under braking, eventually forcing the car's retirement. Clark's new 43/2 overheated, but rejoined the race after the nosecone was removed to admit more cooling air to the radiator. Then the fuel injection failed. There were no Ferraris, so Pedro Rodriguez ran out a convincing winner in the Cooper-Maserati ahead of the local Cooper-Climax of John Love, and John Surtees in the new V12 Honda.

Lotus had hoped the DFV would be ready for the next race, Monaco in early May, but as we've seen the first engines were not delivered until the end of April and Lotus was forced to rely on the old 33s in Monte Carlo. Clark's Tasman-winning car with its 2.0-litre Climax V8 broke its rear suspension, but Hill had a 2.1-litre BRM-engined Lotus 33 which he managed to bring to the finish in second place despite a slipping clutch, broken chassis and deranged suspension. Denny Hulme's Brabham-Repco won a race marred by Ferrari team leader Lorenzo Bandini's death in a fiery crash.

Clark was now a tax exile, spending most of his time in Bermuda or in a flat in Paris that he shared with journalist Gerard 'Jabby' Crombac. The limited time he could spend in the UK each year was almost entirely spoken for by the British GP meeting, which meant he had to give up saloon car racing and could not play a role in the development of the Lotus 49/Cosworth DFV package. In any case, Cosworth was keen to iron out any early bugs before involving the Team Lotus drivers. Initial tests were performed by Mike Costin and Dick Scammell, first using the runway at Hethel and later moving to the Snetterton circuit. There, Costin found that the rear suspension radius rod mounting points on the monocoque failed under the influence of Snetterton's bumpy concrete surface, and 'top hat' reinforcing sections had to be introduced inside the tub to strengthen the mountings.

LEFT: *Early DFVs suffered from internal breathing problems, and ugly external breather tubes were added as a temporary fix. Here, the external breathers are visible on the right-hand cam cover of the DFV in Hill's Lotus 49, which is being studied by Keith Duckworth.*

BELOW: *Brabham provided tough opposition for the new Cosworth-engined Lotuses in 1967. The simple, reliable Repco engine powered them to World Championships in 1966 and 1967.*

RIGHT: *After a troubled Zandvoort practice session Jim Clark had qualified unusually far down the grid, in eighth place. Colin Chapman delivers final instructions to his pensive driver…*

BELOW: *…while Keith Duckworth talks to the press.*

After Indy qualifying and the Monaco Grand Prix, Graham Hill went to Snetterton for his first tests of the Lotus 49. 'It was the most magnificent looking engine – beautifully designed; it really looked like a piece of modern sculpture,' he later wrote. 'I was tickled pink to be sitting in front of this very modern Grand Prix engine – a V8 developing 400hp… it really had some squirt, compared to the Formula 1 cars I had been driving. Very impressive.'

The Snetterton test was little more than a basic shakedown. Hill's car still needed work before it would be ready for the rearranged debut at Zandvoort early in June, while Clark's 49 was still in-build. The Scot saw the car for the first time at Zandvoort, on the Thursday night before practice for the Grand Prix; he hadn't even had a seat fitting, though by then the Lotus mechanics had a good idea how he wanted a car set up. The following day, in the first practice session, Clark drove the 49 for the first time, and that would be the first time his car had turned a wheel in anger… Even so, he finished the first Friday practice session in eighth place, and he was gradually getting used to the DFV's power delivery. Accelerating along the straight in fourth gear Clark found the Lotus was spinning its rear wheels, and he was constantly correcting the car's direction. Hill, meanwhile, was back in 14th after spending much of the session making adjustments to the pedals in his car. Following gearbox swaps to change the ratios, both Lotuses were in the top six on the timesheet for the second of the three sessions that day, and in the final session Hill extended the 49 for the first time with a rousing lap nearly two seconds faster than before. Clark was less happy, complaining that there was something wrong with the feel of his Lotus, but neither he nor his mechanics could pinpoint the problem.

The next day Clark took 49/R2 out again for the qualifying session, but he was soon back in the pits; the car still didn't feel right, and he refused to drive it again until the problem was found. Eventually, the mechanics found the right-rear hub carrier had been split by the ball-race that had broken up. Clark's mechanical sensitivity had warned of a problem long before the mechanics had been able to find evidence of it. Clark lost most of the session while the hub was being changed, and could do nothing but watch as Hill and Dan Gurney traded times – despite some electrical problems on Hill's Lotus and an oil leak from Gurney's Eagle. The Eagle had now moved on from a 2.7-litre Climax FPF to the new Weslake V12, possibly the most

powerful and certainly one of the best looking of the early 3.0-litre Grand Prix engines. Gurney was satisfied with a 1:25.1 lap, nearly three seconds faster than the pole-sitting Brabham-Repco the previous year, which he was convinced had bested the Lotus-Ford challenge. Graham Hill had other ideas. 'I got back in my car and went straight out and equalled this, doing two or three laps at about the same speed,' he wrote later. 'On my last lap, which was also the last lap of practice, I did 1:24.6 – which set everybody talking. It was a real bit of gamesmanship of course and also a very exciting finish to an exciting practice session.'

On race day the track was damp from overnight rain. Gurney lined up alongside Hill on the front row, along with Jack Brabham. Row two was occupied by Jochen Rindt and Pedro Rodriguez in the Cooper-Maseratis and John Surtees in the Honda RA273. Clark's Lotus was back on row three, sandwiched between the Brabham of Denny Hulme and the V12 Ferrari of Chris Amon. When the flag fell, Hill surged into the lead chased by Brabham, while Hulme and Surtees had been forced to avoid an official who was wandering about on the grid as the race started! The Lotus pulled out a two-second lead to Brabham, who was heading a nose-to-tail group which

Team Lotus's two drivers and their Lotus 49s in the Dutch Grand Prix, Clark in number 5 with the while helmet peak, and the much taller Graham Hill in number 6 with his famous London Rowing Club helmet colours. Note how the nose of Hill's 49 appears to be drooping, indicating that the Londoner is hard on the brakes, while at the same point in the corner, Clark is already back on the power.

included Rindt's bulky Cooper, Gurney's lightweight 'titanium' Eagle, Clark in the other Lotus, Hulme's BT20 Brabham and Amon's Ferrari. Then Gurney dropped out of the pack on lap seven, calling at the pits for attention to the fuel injection system, but completing only one more lap before retiring the Eagle-Weslake. Soon after, the Lotus pit crew was shocked to see Brabham flash by in the lead, and no sign of Hill. Eventually, the Lotus appeared, coasting, and Graham pushed it the final few yards into the pits. The engine had died, and before that Hill had been aware of a loud ticking noise. One of the timing gears for the camshafts had thrown its teeth and the camshaft drive had failed.

After losing so much time in practice, Clark had not had the chance to set up his car for the dusty Zandvoort track. Hill's choice of tyres and rear springs had been applied to Clark's car, and the double World Champion had spent the early part of the race getting used to the new set-up. But now he was able to open up the Lotus, taking second place from Rindt on lap 15 and sweeping past Brabham to take the lead a lap later. 'Black Jack' hung on to the speeding Lotus for a while, but by one-third distance Clark had opened out a five-second lead and by two-thirds distance he was a comfortable 18

seconds ahead. On a drying track the flying Scotsman lapped everybody up to and including Mike Parkes in the Ferrari in fifth place, and on lap 67 he set a new lap record of 1:28.08 which would have been fastest enough to qualify for pole position in the previous year's Grand Prix. Brabham had settled for second, and all that could come between Clark and victory was a repeat of the failure which had sidelined Hill. Fortunately, Clark's car was fresher than Hill's, which had clocked up plenty of testing miles – but then, Clark's car was so new it was unproven. Suddenly, as Clark began the 84th of 90 laps, the DFV engine note changed as the Lotus flashed past the pits. Was Clark's Cosworth engine about to fail the same way as Hill's had? The Lotus was lapping a second or so below its best, but on the next lap Team Lotus mechanics noted that the engine note was now crisp and Clark had not signalled a problem. He had simply lifted off to preserve the car and the engine, knowing that Brabham was well beaten. The Ford-Cosworth DFV had won its debut race, and Jim Clark had won the Dutch Grand Prix and recorded the fastest race lap in a car he had not even sat in, let alone driven, prior to the race meeting.

Chapman and Duckworth appeared on the podium

RIGHT: *Using Hill's settings, Clark gradually made his way through the field. By lap 15 he was ahead of Jochen Rindt's cumbersome Cooper-Maserati and in pursuit of the leading Brabham.*

BELOW: *Clark lapped everyone up to fifth place and set a new lap record. A Lotus mechanic holds out a pit board to show the double World Champion his lead over Brabham, while a dapper Colin Chapman waits for the Lotus to start another lap.*

with Jim Clark to celebrate a dazzling victory. Ford's Walter Hayes and Harley Copp were also present, having flown out from Southend in a light plane, but they maintained a low profile. As Team Lotus and Cosworth congratulated each other, the Ford men slipped away to catch their plane from Schipol airport – stopping along the way to buy two bottles of beer, which they consumed in the car, to toast Clark's success.

But the victory had not been as easy as it might have appeared to the thousands who watched the green and yellow Lotus finish more than 30 seconds ahead of the green and gold Brabham. Throughout the race Clark had been troubled by a recalcitrant clutch, and towards the end the Lotus 49's brakes had become less and less responsive. Nor was the engine in pristine condition; back in the pits an unhealthy rattle emanated from the front end of the engine, and a subsequent strip down proved that Clark's DFV had suffered from the same problem as Hill's – two teeth were missing from one of the camshaft timing gears. Unfortunately for Hill, the two missing teeth were adjacent, and that was enough to break drive to the camshafts. Fortunately for Clark, the two missing teeth were separated by one good one, which was just enough to keep the cams turning...

Triumph for Clark, and a victory for the DFV in its first race. But the Lotus was not in the rudest health: the timing gears were breaking up, the clutch was failing, and the brakes were disappearing.

ABOVE: *Clark brings the victorious Lotus 49 back to the Zandvoort pits. It was the first of four wins for Clark in the Lotus 49 in 1967.*

RIGHT: *On the victory podium Jim Clark celebrates, while Keith Duckworth (on Clark's right) can't quite believe it – but Colin Chapman has seen it all before.*

OPPOSITE: *Hill's Belgian Grand Prix was brief. He stalled the Lotus at the start, and retired with gearbox problems on the third lap.*

Both DFVs were returned to Cosworth for rebuilds in preparation for the Belgian Grand Prix two weeks later. With only two complete DFVs in existence that meant Lotus could do no testing on the 49s, so they arrived at Spa-Francorchamps in much the same specification that they had run at Zandvoort. The opposition was much the same, too, although Brabham had switched to the new BT24 and given the old BT19 to Hulme. Friday practice saw Clark and Hill post times of 3:31.5 and 3:32.9 respectively for the 8.8 mile circuit. Clark went a few tenths faster, and then recorded a scorching 3:29.0. Dan Gurney's rapid Eagle-Weslake was again the only car to approach the speed of the Lotus-Fords, and Gurney posted a 3:31.2 lap right at the end of the session.

In the final qualifying session the following day, Clark recorded a 3:28.1 lap to put pole position beyond the reach of Gurney, who would line up second, and Hill, who would be third following engine woes. Both Lotus drivers tried 'air deflectors' under the noses of their Lotus 49s during practice, to quell lift on the high-speed Spa circuit, but both found they caused instability and neither car had an air deflector fitted for the race.

Clark leapt into an early lead ahead of Rindt's Cooper-Maserati, while Hill was stranded on the startline, apparently having failed to follow the correct starting procedure. The DFV had to be started by spinning the engine on the starter before switching on the ignition – if the ignition was switched on first the engine would often fire prematurely, turn backwards and stop, and under such treatment the starter would eventually overheat. On Hill's car the battery was changed and the engine started, and the Lotus was sent on its way more than a minute behind the leaders. Not that it made much difference as Hill was back in the pits on lap two with clutch trouble, and out on lap three with gearbox problems.

Clark continued to lap two seconds faster than the opposition until lap 12, when he brought the Lotus into the pits with a misfire. The porcelain core had blown out of one of the spark plugs. The problem was diagnosed and the offending plug replaced in two minutes, and Clark rejoined in seventh place. He was back three laps later with the same problem, and by the time he rejoined the race he was a lap down on the leaders. The Lotus was also suffering clutch trouble again and Clark was forcing the selector lever into the gear positions, which eventually damaged the gearchange linkage leaving him with only first, third and fifth gears available! He eventually finished sixth, and Dan Gurney secured a popular win in the Eagle-Weslake. The Autolite plugs which Ford had insisted were used (Autolite was a Ford brand) were initially blamed for Clark's troubles, but Autolite reckoned the 10mm plugs were being overtightened, and issued torque wrenches pre-set to the correct tightening torque. The failures miraculously disappeared…

Team Lotus missed Friday practice for the next championship round, the French Grand Prix, due to a delay in customs at Dieppe. The race was held that year on the Le Mans Bugatti circuit, which used the Le Mans pits and the Dunlop Bridge corner, and then branched off into an infield car park where the track snaked backwards and forwards before rejoining the main circuit just before the pits. Drivers called it a 'Mickey Mouse' track, journalists referred to the 'Grand Prix of the Car Parks'. It was an unhappy event for Team Lotus and during qualifying both Lotuses struggled with mysterious

misfires. Clark was a frustrated fourth but Hill's engine cured itself right at the end of the session, and he turned in a remarkable lap that stole pole position from Jack Brabham by a tenth of a second.

Clark's car was worked on into the night, and when the mechanics eventually felt it was running cleanly Clark gave the unsilenced 49 a blast down the main road to check everything was working. 'You can imagine what a Grand Prix car developing 400bhp sounds like in the dead of night,' wrote Graham Hill later, 'very antisocial.' Come Sunday, Hill took an early lead but after 13 laps he was out with final-drive failure. Clark lasted a further ten laps before his Lotus suffered the same problem; the torque of the DFV was such that the loads generated between the crownwheel and pinion were causing the final-drive housing to flex, and the resulting misalignment of the gears was leading to wear and failure. ZF came up with a solution: cast iron plates either side of the final-drive unit, held together by long cross bolts. It was heavy, but effective.

Brabham recorded a one–two victory in France, with Denny Hulme second to his team leader, both of them in the latest Ron Tauranac-designed Brabham BT24s. Two weeks later, at Silverstone for the British Grand Prix, the two Brabhams battled for pole position with the Lotuses, which were recovering from more misfires in the first practice session. Overnight, Keith Duckworth had traced the source of the misfire to an unnecessary bleed hole in a fuel system bypass pipe, which he blocked by tapering an ordinary pin and hammering it into the tiny hole until it sealed. Clark quickly lapped more than a second faster than anyone else, and soon Hill had also recorded times faster than the Brabhams. But on the way back to the pits after setting his fastest time, Hill suddenly found himself a passenger as the Lotus turned sharp right into the retaining wall, ripping off the right front suspension and denting the tub. The pick-up point for the lower left-hand radius rod had failed as Hill braked to enter the pit lane, and the rear wheel had turned outwards and steered the car into the wall.

Clark's mechanic Allan McCall was left to 'cobble up' a stronger mounting bracket on 49/R2 while the rest of the team was flown back to Hethel. There, a new tub, 49/R3, was sitting partly built and Chapman hoped a concerted effort would get it raceworthy overnight. The forlorn 49/R1 was loaded onto the team's transporter and driven back to supply necessary parts. Stripping R1 and building R3 took all night, and continued in the paddock at Silverstone the following day – ex-mechanic Hill pitching in to help ready the car. R3 looked rather odd as there were no spares for the latest wide windscreen or the glassfibre nose cones – so R3 ran with an old-style narrow screen and an aluminium nose, which was actually a pattern that had been made for moulding glassfibre nose cones! In *Motor Sport*, Denis Jenkinson quoted Colin Chapman: 'Sixteen of us did three weeks' work overnight.'

Remarkably, Hill's car was ready to run by the appointed start time of 3pm, and because his approach had always been to test in detail and record everything, R1's settings were easily transferred to R3. Despite sitting on the startline in a car which had never turned a wheel, Hill could expect R3 to be set up reasonably well for Silverstone's fast, open corners. Clark led away from the start but Brabham got ahead of Hill until the Englishman felt more confident in his 'bitsa' Lotus. Hill re-passed Brabham on lap nine, and set about catching and then passing his team-mate. Hill retained the lead until lap 55 when the Lotus suddenly slowed coming out of Becketts Corner, its left rear wheel leaning inwards at the top. During the frantic overnight build, an Allen bolt holding the transverse link of the rear suspension had not be properly tightened, and had fallen out. A replacement

Hill explains what went wrong, while Chapman updates his lap chart. The simple pit garages at Spa are a far cry from the palatial splendour of today's F1 facilities.

was quickly found and Hill was on his way in less than a minute, but combined with his slow tour to the pits he had lost two laps on the leaders and was now lying seventh. He was soon catching Surtees's sixth-placed Honda, but to no avail; on lap 64 the engine failed, and Hill coasted to a halt on the outside of Copse Corner. That left Clark to win as he pleased, Denny Hulme finishing 13 seconds behind with Amon and Brabham the only other drivers on the same lap as the winner.

Early on, the drivers had revealed how the DFV was tricky to drive thanks to its savage torque delivery. The engine suffered something of a flat spot in the middle of its rev-range, around 5,000rpm, and then came out of the flat spot with a bang around 6,500rpm. Clark likened it to suddenly having a second engine come on stream. Torque and power climbed rapidly over a small part of the engine speed range, making a DFV-powered Lotus tricky to handle unless the driver was aware of the step in the power curve. To aid the drivers Colin Chapman devised a progressive throttle linkage, and Maurice Philippe turned his ideas into working drawings. The system was fitted to the cars from the French Grand Prix and now, as Team Lotus prepared for the German Grand Prix at the Nürburgring, the linkage was revised

to improve control still further. Another change to the engine was the adoption of a new ignition box within the engine 'V', above the throttle slides, a modification made by Cosworth to neaten the engine installation in the car. Previously, the ignition coil and control boxes had been in an exposed position on top of the final drive unit. Magnesium reinforcing plates now held the final drive units together, in place of the heavy cast iron plates.

On the chassis side, Hill's wrecked 49/R1 was rebuilt to the same specification as the hurriedly assembled R3, with the latest internal reinforcements to the monocoque, longer fairings for the front suspension rocker arms and a larger access panel above the driver's knees. The errant Allen bolt in the suspension was replaced by a stud and the suspension link was secured by a self-locking nut, with a wired locknut for the ultimate in security. Another feature of R3, retrospectively added to the earlier monocoques, was intended to avoid damage to the rear bulkhead of the monocoque from the bolt on the nose of the crankshaft. An indentation was added to the bulkhead to ensure clearance between it and the engine even when the fuel and air in the fuel tank behind the bulkhead warmed up and expanded, pushing the bulkhead backwards.

At the Nürburgring, Clark found himself suffering brake trouble, because the brake cooling was too good. The large ventilated front discs, out in the airstream, were being overcooled and as a result the pads were glazing. Solid discs were fitted to Clark's car, while Hill's was fitted with softer brake pads. Unfortunately for Hill, his car only managed half a lap before the gearbox seized due to lack of oil, and he had to switch from R1, his rebuilt Silverstone car, to the spare chassis R3. Jacky Ickx provided the story of the day during Friday practice, putting the cat among the pigeons with a lap in 8:14 in a Matra Formula 2 car with Cosworth FVA power, some 10 seconds faster than most of the Formula 1 machinery had managed. Only Hulme, in the Brabham-Repco, was faster, and then only by half a second.

Hill crashed R3 heavily in the final session on Saturday, misjudging a braking point on the way to Breidscheid. R3 ran up the bank and spun back on to the track minus its gearbox and left-side suspension. The damage was too severe to repair, so R1 was wheeled out and rebuilt for Hill to use in the race. Meanwhile, Hill borrowed Clark's race car to complete the last of the required five practice laps, which with all his dramas, he had so far failed to do. Chapman enjoined him to bring the machine back in one piece, which he succeeded in

Silverstone, '67: the flag drops and Clark's Lotus sprints into the lead, ahead of Hill's spare-parts special, built up overnight after a suspension failure pitched him into the wall in practice, destroying his race car. Behind them, Amon's Ferrari has jumped ahead of the Brabhams, and Dan Gurney's Eagle is being attacked from both sides by Cooper-Maseratis – squeezing Rindt's perilously close to the wall. The two Lotuses disputed the lead until Hill's Cosworth engine failed, leaving Clark to win easily.

doing to everyone's relief. Clark had already secured pole position with a scorching 8:04.1 lap, although he still didn't think he had extracted the best from the car. Hill's disrupted practice left him back on the fourth row between Jo Siffert's Cooper-Maserati and Hubert Hahne's 2.0-litre Lola-BMW.

Clark took the lead from the start, chased by the Brabham of Hulme and the Eagles of McLaren and Gurney, but the Lotus 49 was not handling well. After four laps he relinquished the lead and crawled back to the pits, where a buckled front suspension rocker and a punctured rear tyre were discovered. Hill pitted with a loose front wheel nut, then rejoined the race only to retire when the bolt connecting one of the rear suspension brackets to its DFV cylinder head went missing, and the suspension was left to sink inwards. Gurney's Eagle-Weslake looked certain to win but a driveshaft universal joint failed late in the race, leaving Denny Hulme to head a Brabham one–two. Once again, the Lotus-Fords had shown unmatched speed in qualifying but had failed to translate that into a win on race day. Despite that, Walter Hayes could see that once reliability had been built into the Lotuses they would dominate completely, and he discussed with

Colin Chapman the idea of releasing the DFV engines to other teams for 1968. The original contract gave Lotus exclusive use of the Cosworth motor until the end of the 1968 season, but Chapman agreed with Hayes: perhaps he, too, could see that utter domination by one team was not good for the long-term future of the sport.

At the inaugural Canadian Grand Prix at Mosport, at the end of August, the Lotuses again flattered to deceive. Occasional misfires which had plagued the DFVs had now been traced to sediment in the fuel system, and gauze filters like those used on the Climax-engined cars had been added, solving the problem. After trying Goodyear tyres in practice the Lotuses reverted to Firestones for the qualifying session, during which Clark got down to 1:22.4 and Hill 1:22.7, with no other cars beating 1:23.0. Both drivers were comfortably inside the previous best practice lap seen at Mosport, a 1:22.9 by Jim Hall's Chaparral sports car. Local driver Eppie Wietzes ran a third Lotus, 49/R1, and qualified at the back of the grid despite having no previous experience of a 3.0-litre F1 car. Clark led the wet/dry race and recorded the fastest lap, but eventually water got into the DFV's ignition system and shorted it out, and Wietzes's car had similar troubles. Hill kept going despite

Graham Hill chats to Keith Duckworth in the pits at Monza in 1967.

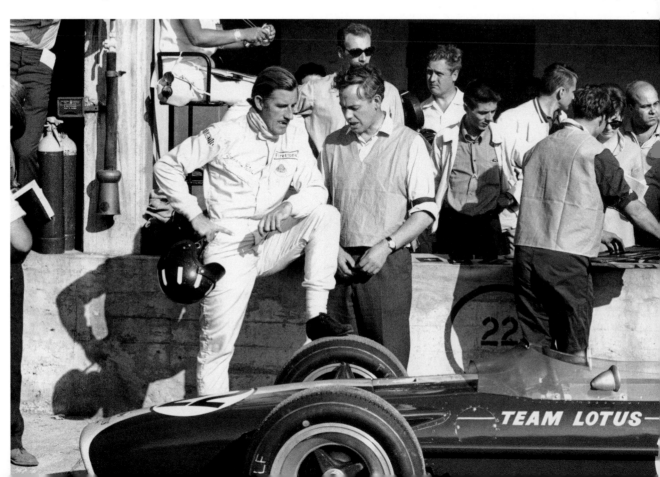

a spin to finish fourth – the first time he had completed a race with DFV power. Bruce McLaren's new McLaren M5A had a BRM V12 but, bizarrely, no alternator, and predictably had to stop for a fresh battery. But for the stop McLaren might have won the race, which instead, was another Brabham benefit, this time headed by 'Black Jack' himself.

From Canada the F1 circus re-crossed the Atlantic for the European Grand Prix at Monza. Jim Clark put his usual Lotus 49/R2 on pole position early in the qualifying session with a lap of 1:28.5, with Jack Brabham and Bruce McLaren just behind after some crafty slipstreaming. Thirty minutes into the session rain washed away any hopes of faster laps, leaving Hill eighth in 49/R3, just ahead of Surtees in the new Lola-based Honda, which had quickly acquired the nickname 'Hondola'. Local boy Giancarlo Baghetti was at the back of the field in Lotus 49/R1. The top half of the grid was tightly congested, with the Brabham-Repcos, McLaren's BRM-powered car and Gurney's Eagle-Weslake all competitive once again. Ferrari had entered a lone car for Amon; a new chassis with a new version of the 3.0-litre V12 engine, now sporting four-valve cylinder heads. The prospects were for an exciting race.

The start was the usual Monza chaos. The drivers formed up on what was theoretically a 'dummy' grid, and a '30 seconds' board was shown. The usual procedure was that the starter would call the field forward to the start line a few seconds before the appointed time, then drop a flag to start the race. Nothing happened until the 30 seconds were up, when the official waved a green flag which should have invited the drivers to move forward to the startline – but Brabham and others interpreted that as the start and were off, with the rest of the pack, including a bewildered Clark, chasing. Hill profited from the confusion, briefly holding second place and then slotting in behind a hard-charging Gurney, with Clark behind in fourth. By the end of the first lap Gurney had put the Eagle ahead of the Brabham and a lap later Clark took Hill and Brabham to assume second place. Clark passed Gurney on lap three, then the American's challenge ended with a dead Weslake engine after a connecting-rod bolt let go. Shortly after, Scarfiotti brought the second Eagle in with damaged timing gears.

Clark had a second in hand from Hill and the two Brabhams, Hulme now ahead of his team owner and catching the Lotuses. But Clark was in trouble with an

Surtees and Brabham sprint for the line at the end of an eventful Italian Grand Prix. The Honda (right) won by just a fifth of a second. Clark's Lotus had recovered from a puncture to regain the lead, only to run out of fuel on the last lap.

ABOVE *Early problems with the DFV centred on the troublesome timing gears and an inadequate oil breather system. As a temporary cure for the breathing problems Cosworth added unsightly, though effective, external breather tubes from the right-hand cam box cover.*

OPPOSITE *Graham Hill heads out of the Kyalami pits in practice for the South African Grand Prix, en route to a front-row grid slot and second place at the finish. Already, sponsorship decals are more in evidence, but soon Lotuses will adopt full Gold Leaf livery.*

ill-handling car, and the drivers behind could see why: the right-hand rear tyre was punctured. Jack Brabham slithered inside the Lotus going into the South Curve and gesticulated wildly at the offending tyre, and Clark disappeared into the pits for new rubber. He rejoined in 15th place, not far behind the leading trio of Hulme, Brabham and Hill on the road, but actually a whole lap down. Clark passed Bonnier, Ligier and Ickx, then caught the leading cars on lap 21. In a couple of laps he was past all three, Hulme slotting in behind the Lotus for a tow which took him past Hill and into the lead.

Soon, Clark was pulling away from the leading group at record pace, and was past Spence and Siffert. At the front of the race Hill repassed Hulme, the Brabham suffering from a failed head-gasket and loss of cooling water. Brabham was also slow, as the Repco's throttles had briefly stuck wide open and buzzed the engine. Clark streaked away with Hill in his slipstream, the pair of them circulating two seconds a lap faster than anyone else. Clark passed Rindt's Cooper-Maserati for fourth place on lap 53 and set off after Surtees, who in turn was catching Brabham. Hill had almost a lap in his pocket, but his run of bad luck wasn't over yet: on lap 59 his engine failed. 'There was an almighty bang and I managed to coast around the corner and into the pits,'

he remembered later. 'The crankshaft had broken.' Hill's forlorn R3 joined Baghetti's R1 in retirement, the Italian's engine having broken a camshaft on lap 51.

Clark sailed past Surtees, who stuck close behind the Lotus to use the tow to his advantage. As the leading group went past the pits to begin lap 61 Clark was ready to take the lead from Brabham – after making up an entire lap on the leaders following that pit stop to change a wheel. Surtees fought past Brabham to take second place, then with barely a lap to go Clark's Lotus faltered. Surtees and Brabham surged past. Brabham attempted to outbrake Surtees into the Parabolica, but slid wide on cement dust lining the inside of the corner following Hill's engine failure. The Honda took a breathless victory barely a car's length ahead, while Clark's Lotus coasted over the line to finish third. Officially the cause was revealed as a fuel pick-up problem, the pumps struggling to find the last few litres, although Chapman always wanted to run as light on fuel as possible to minimise weight. Clark had used the DFV harder than ever before in his pursuit of the leaders, and it seems likely that the Lotus simply ran out of fuel.

The next round of the championship was the United States Grand Prix at Watkins Glen, a financially attractive race for the European teams thanks to a prize fund of more than $103,000 with travel expenses paid for by the organisers. Team Lotus brought its three 49s (the spare car to be used by Mexican driver Moises Solana), there was the usual pair of Brabhams, three H16 BRMs for Jackie Stewart, Mike Spence and Chris Irwin, McLaren's BRM-engined car and the 'Hondola' driven by Surtees. The All-American Racers team was lacking raceworthy engines after two failures at Monza, Weslake's apparent inability to supply engines with interchangeable components hampering the rebuilds, and they arrived with just a single Eagle for Dan Gurney. There were two 36-valve Cooper-Maseratis, for Jochen Rindt and Jacky Ickx. One was fitted with the usual twin distributors and two plugs per cylinder, but Keith Duckworth was amused to find the second engine had no less than three spark plugs per cylinder, with a third distributor at the back of the engine. Duckworth suggested that there must be something seriously wrong somewhere if more than one spark was needed to make it go bang…

By the close of practice on Friday, Clark had set the pace with a blistering lap of 1:06.80, with Hill a couple of tenths slower and the pair of them the only drivers to break 1:08. Towards the end of the Saturday session Clark reduced his time to 1:06.07, then Hill went out and

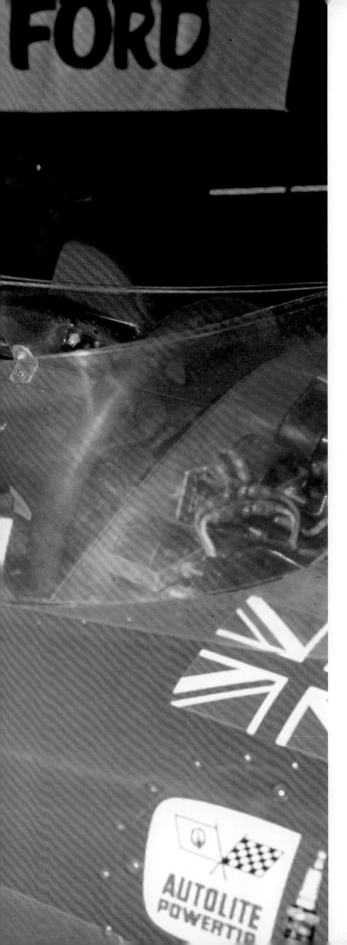

quickly got down to Clark's times, then popped in a lap at 1:05.48 to secure pole position by half a second and claim the $1,000 qualifying prize. What was obvious to Walter Hayes was that Hill and Clark would have a similar battle in the race and might take each other off in the process, or work the engines hard enough to fail, and a Ford victory on home soil might be lost despite the Lotus-Fords being clearly superior to the competition. That night Hayes summoned both drivers and flipped a coin for the race, Hill called and won the toss, and it was agreed that Hill would win at Watkins Glen. As a consolation prize, Clark would have preference at the next race in Mexico.

Hill took an early lead in the race, and Gurney got past Clark to run second until the Lotus re-passed him on lap eight. The two Lotuses ran nose to tail, with Amon's Ferrari coming up through the field to catch them up. Hill's car was now suffering clutch problems, and eventually Clark was given a signal to pass his team-mate. Hill's problems were intermittent, and when everything was working he proved the Lotus-Ford's pace by breaking the lap record twice, but in between he was forced to give up second place to Amon's charging Ferrari until the V12 ran out of oil and seized. Hill soldiered on with a minute or so in hand over Hulme and Siffert, but up at the front Clark was having dramas of his own: two laps from the end the top transverse link in the right rear suspension failed, allowing the rear wheel to fall inwards at the top. Two very slow laps later Clark had crawled across the line to win, with Hill just six seconds behind in second place. One headline called the Lotus 'The Ultimate Race Car – It Breaks at the Finish Line!' Inevitably, Hill was less than pleased when he realised how close he had come to winning a race that by prior agreement had been his, but Clark apologised and Hayes, at least, had his Lotus-Ford one–two in the bag.

Moises Solana again took over the spare Lotus at the Mexican Grand Prix three weeks later. At first he drove 49/R1, with Clark in his regular R2 and Hill in R3. When a routine oil change showed evidence of a bearing failure, R1 was given a fresh engine – at which point Clark took the car over, and Solana was given R2. Clark put the car on pole without too much trouble, aborting a lap which would probably have been even faster to avoid providing Denny Hulme with a tow along the pits straight. Chris Amon's 48-valve Ferrari was second, followed by Gurney and Hill. The start of the race proved farcical: the starter jiggled the flag and a wrong-footed Clark was so slow

Early in 1968, Lotus fitted the 49s with short-stroke 2.5-litre Cosworth engines, designated DFWs, to compete in the Tasman series. Jim Clark, the eventual champion, looks relaxed and happy in the cockpit of his Lotus, now carrying the red, white and gold colours of its Gold Leaf sponsor.

After Clark's death at Hockenheim, and then Mike Spence's at Indianapolis, Graham Hill did an enormous amount to pull Team Lotus together. A win at the Spanish Grand Prix was just the tonic that was needed.

away that he was rammed by Gurney's Eagle, one of the Lotus exhaust pipes puncturing the Eagle radiator and putting Gurney out straight away. Clark got away third and was soon past Amon and Hill to take a lead he would never relinquish. On lap 13 Solana dropped out with a front suspension failure (in the car Clark had expected to run in the race) while Hill was out soon after with a driveshaft failure. Nevertheless, Clark never looked troubled and finished more than a minute ahead of Brabham and the new World Champion, Denny Hulme.

Although the World Championship was over, the season was not yet at an end. Team Lotus drove down to Jarama for the non-championship Madrid Grand Prix, where Clark and Hill finished one–two in a field largely composed of Formula 2 machinery. The 1968 season was just a few weeks away, starting on 1 January with the South African Grand Prix at Kyalami. Cosworth was busy producing a new DFV specification known as the '8 series' (8 standing for 1968) and ensuring it had sufficient stocks of engines and parts to support wider use of the DFV in 1968. Ken Tyrrell's Matra International team had signed up to use Cosworth power, as had the McLaren Racing Organisation – where World Champion Denny Hulme lined up alongside Bruce McLaren. Customer DFVs were available at £7,500 a unit, and barring untoward problems, each engine could be expect to last around 600 racing miles before needing a £500 rebuild followed by a £200 dynamometer run.

At Kyalami, for the first round of the 1968 championship, Clark tried Dunlop tyres on his new Lotus 49/R4 before reverting to the usual Firestones. His 1:21.6 lap took pole position in front of Hill, ahead of the new Cosworth-powered Matra MS9 in the hands of Jackie Stewart – so new it was still unpainted – followed by Brabham-Repco new-boy Jochen Rindt, and Brabham himself. At the start it was Stewart who got away best, but his lead lasted only a lap before Clark came through and then gradually drove away from the pack, setting a new lap record in the process. Hill, meanwhile, had recovered from a poor start to snatch second away from Stewart's Matra, which broke a connecting rod just after half distance. Lotus-Ford finished first and second, Clark winning his 25th Grand Prix to break Fangio's record.

Cosworth had agreed to provide Lotus with a 2.5-litre version of the DFV engine, known as the DFW, for use in the Tasman series during the spring of 1968. Very little development work was carried out: standard DFVs were simply fitted with short-stroke crankshafts to reduce

the capacity to 2,495cc, and longer connecting rods to keep friction down and the compression ratio up. The resulting power output was around 350bhp. Fitted with the DFW-spec engine the Tasman cars – the usual Lotus 49 chassis R1 and R2 – were now known as 49Ts, and Clark's car was in action the week after the South African Grand Prix, at Pukekohe in New Zealand. It qualified on pole position but then retired from the race with seized valvegear. A week later at Levin, Clark again put the Lotus on pole but made a rare driving error in the race and retired with deranged suspension, in what turned out to be the last race where Lotus ran their 49s in the classic green and yellow livery. For the third Tasman race, the Lady Wigram Trophy, Clark's R2 was painted in the red, white and gold colours of the Gold Leaf cigarette brand, after Colin Chapman and Geoffrey Kent of John Player had struck a deal for Players to sponsor Team Lotus. Clark won comfortably from Amon's 2.4-litre Ferrari, but had to settle for second a week later in the Teretonga Trophy after a spin in torrential rain.

The Tasman series then moved to Australia, where Clark was joined by Graham Hill in R1. The pair finished one–two at Surfers Paradise and again at Warwick Farm, then Clark won a race-long battle with Amon's new four-valve Ferrari at Sandown Park. What nobody knew was that it was to be the last win for Clark in the Lotus-Ford. The final round of the series was at the Longford street circuit in Tasmania. In heavy rain Piers Courage led the way in a nimble Cosworth FVA-powered McLaren F2 car and Clark could only finish fifth, but that was enough to wrap up the Tasman series. The cars returned to Europe (where the short-stroke DFWs were converted back to regular DFVs) and Graham Hill took a new chassis, R5, to the Race of Champions. Technical niggles and an argument over sponsor's logos disrupted practice, then the race ended with a failed driveshaft. Just a few weeks later, at Hockenheim, Clark's FVA-powered Lotus F2 car left the road in mysterious circumstances and crashed into a tree. The popular Scot never had a chance.

The motor racing world was shocked, and Team Lotus was devastated. While work sombrely continued on a revised Lotus 49, and the new 56 turbine car for Indianapolis, a single Lotus entry at Silverstone for the non-championship BRDC International Trophy saw Hill qualify only sixth, the field headed by Denny Hulme in the DFV-engined McLaren. Hill's race ended after 52 laps with a fuel leak, while Jo Siffert in R2 (loaned to Rob Walker after Walker's own R4 had been lost in a workshop fire) retired with a clutch failure. Still worse

was to come. Jackie Stewart had been drafted in to replace Clark in the 56 turbine car, but injured his wrist in a Formula 2 accident, so his former BRM team-mate Mike Spence was recruited. Exactly a month after Clark's death, Spence put one of the 56s into the wall, and was unlucky to be hit on the head by a front wheel which had been torn off in the impact. He never regained consciousness.

Morale inside Team Lotus hit an all-time low. Colin Chapman went home before the Indy 500 began, and didn't reappear until after the Spanish Grand Prix. The new Lotus 49B was there, but on Chapman's instructions it was not used, and Hill reverted to R1. He qualified sixth, behind Amon's pole-sitting Ferrari, Rodriguez's V12 BRM, the Cosworth-powered McLarens and the Cosworth-powered Matra MS10 of Jean-Pierre Beltoise (deputising for the injured Jackie Stewart). Amon's pole was the first by a non-Cosworth car since Monaco in 1967, 11 races earlier. The night before the race Graham and Bette Hill took the Lotus team out to the Villa Rosa restaurant in Madrid in a bid to restore morale, but the following day Hill found an even better way to build the spirit in the team, by winning the race comfortably from Hulme's McLaren-Ford after the Ferrari and BRM challenge evaporated. It was his first win for the team.

The 49B adopted a Hewland gearbox, the FG400, and revised rear suspension. The suspension forces were now fed through a hefty rear cross-member mounted on the final drive, which relieved the DFV cylinder heads of their load. To improve weight distribution a 'saddle' oil tank was mounted over the gearbox, and the latest 12in-wide front wheels were fitted. The car's competition debut came at Monaco, where Hill qualified on pole and led all but three laps to head just five running cars at the finish and record his second Grand Prix win in succession. Although both Lotuses succumbed to driveshaft universal joint failures at Spa, new Lotus number two Jack Oliver was classified fifth and another Cosworth-powered car, a McLaren M7A driven by Bruce himself, won the race. Like the Lotus, the Robin Herd-designed M7A was a 'truncated monocoque' design using the DFV as a stressed chassis member, and the monocoque itself was made from aluminium panels wrapped around steel bulkheads. From the start McLaren opted to use the Hewland DG300 gearbox, which Lotus would later adopt for the 49B in place of the smaller FG400.

Matra's MS10 also followed the pattern of aluminium skins and steel bulkheads, but instead of feeding the

rear suspension loads through the engine and the gearbox the Matra carried its rear suspension on a tubular subframe which fed the loads into the bulkhead behind the driver's shoulders. At Zandvoort, Jackie Stewart donned a plastic support for his damaged wrist and splashed through the rain in his Cosworth-powered Tyrrell Matra to beat Jean-Pierre Beltoise's works Matra MS11, which was powered by the French company's own V12 engine. Jacky Ickx finished third in Belgium, fourth in Holland, then gave the V12 Ferrari the win it was looking for in the wet French Grand Prix at Rouen, the race which claimed the life of Honda driver Jo Schlesser. In practice, Jack Oliver had been lucky to escape unscathed from a 140mph impact with a stone gate post after his bewinged Lotus was unsettled by the slipstream of another car.

The rest of the season would be a DFV benefit. Siffert's Rob Walker Lotus 49B won the British Grand Prix ahead of a pair of Ferraris. Stewart won at the Nürburgring and Watkins Glen, with Hill second on both occasions. Hulme's McLaren won back-to-back races in Italy and Canada and then Hill's Lotus cruised home in the Mexican Grand Prix to secure the Englishman's second world title. DFV-engined cars had won all but one of the season's Grand Prix races: Cosworth domination had begun.

OPPOSITE: Graham Hill acknowledges the applause after his win at Jarama, flanked by a smiling Denny Hulme (second in a DFV-engined McLaren) and a rather glum-looking Brian Redman (third in a Cooper-BRM). Two weeks later Hill would win again, at Monaco.

ABOVE: Ken Tyrrell built a new team around Jackie Stewart in 1968, using Matra chassis and Cosworth DFV engines. Stewart regularly beat the works Matras with their V12 engines.

CHAPTER FIVE

DFV DOMINATION

DFV engines powered more F1 cars than ever in 1969, a season full of developments in chassis technology and aerodynamics. As the focus of development switched from engines to other areas of the car, the Cosworth teams could renew their challenge against potentially more powerful rivals. And there were plenty of Cosworth teams: Lotus, Matra, McLaren and Brabham all fielded DFV-engined cars, leaving only the fading BRMs and fast but unreliable Ferraris to mount any kind of challenge.

Lotus, McLaren and Matra had all realised that the DFV gave them more power than their rear wheels could efficiently cope with. Four-wheel drive looked like a good solution, and had already been tried with some success at Indianapolis. Cosworth also decided to develop a four-wheel drive F1 car of its own, and hired Robin Herd from McLaren to do the chassis design. Lotus already had experience of four-wheel drive with their turbine-powered 56 and 64 Indy cars, which they applied to the DFV-engined 63. Like other DFV-powered four-wheel drive cars, the engine was turned through 180 degrees so that the clutch was right behind the driver, and from there the drive was split forwards and rearwards – in the case of the Lotus and McLaren running down the left-hand side of the car, and down the right-hand side on the Matra and Cosworth.

John Miles and Mario Andretti campaigned the Lotus 63 during 1969, but the advantages of four-wheel drive on fast American oval tracks did not translate into European road racing where it was more important

Fittipaldi stayed with McLaren for 1975, finishing second in the World Championship to Ferrari's Niki Lauda. In the Silverstone pits, 'Emmo' listens while McLaren team boss Teddy Mayer makes a point to his number-one driver.

Contrasting cars and styles in the non-championship Race of Champions at Brands Hatch in 1969. World Champion Graham Hill's Gold Leaf Team Lotus 49B (No. 1) has nose-mounted front wings and Firestone tyres, and a rear oil cooler partially blanked off against the March chill. Brabham No. 5) and Hulme's McLaren (No. 3) have high wings front and rear and characteristically square-shouldered Goodyear tyres.

for the driver to have precise throttle control of the car's attitude in a corner. Matra found a similar story with their MS84, which only managed to score a single point in the hands of Johnny Servoz-Gavin, and that was with drive to the front wheels disabled. McLaren's M9A was abandoned even more quickly, racing just once. Cosworth's car never even made it that far, being withdrawn from the only race where it was entered, at the British Grand Prix. The project was cancelled, and Robin Herd left Cosworth to form March late in 1969.

Meanwhile, a simpler and potentially more effective solution to the traction problem was being introduced. Aerodynamics in motor sport had generally concentrated on reducing drag, but inverted wings to create downforce had occasionally been seen, notably on Michael May's Porsche in the 1950s and more recently Jim Hall's Chaparral 2F sports car. Lotus had dabbled with the idea during the Tasman series early in 1968, using part of a scrap helicopter rotor blade picked up at a local airfield – experiments to determine the optimum angle of attack were carried out by hanging the blade out of the car window on the way back from the airfield! Ferrari and Brabham then introduced wings to Formula 1 at the Belgian Grand Prix, and they were soon adopted

by all the major teams. Tall mounting struts were used to keep the wings out of the 'dirty' air flow around the body of the car, and the downforce generated by the wings was fed directly into the suspension uprights. Some teams had movable wings which could be 'feathered' on the straights, reducing the angle of attack of the wing to minimise drag when maximum downforce was not needed. Matra's wings were electrically operated (using a motor designed for use in a missile!) while Lotus had a more pragmatic solution using a bungee-cord system connected to an extra pedal in the cockpit, which the driver pressed on the straights.

It was two accidents involving the Lotus 49s of Graham Hill and Jochen Rindt which would lead to a ban on high wings. At the Spanish Grand Prix in 1969 Hill's car crashed after the rear wing buckled, suddenly removing the downforce from the rear wheels. Moments later the wing on Rindt's car failed in exactly the same way, at exactly the same spot – which meant the luckless Austrian not only bounced off the Armco barriers but also cannoned into Hill's wrecked car. While still in hospital recovering from his injuries Rindt penned an open letter detailing his opposition to the use of wings. At Monaco the scrutineers decided not to accept wings,

JOCHEN RINDT ON WINGS

This is an open letter to all people who are interested in Formula 1 racing. I want to demonstrate a few points about the aerofoils which at the moment are used on most of the F1 cars, in order to convince the so-called experts that they should be banned.

Basically I have two reasons why I am against them:

1. Wings have nothing to do with a motor car. They are completely out of place and will never be used on a road-going production car. Please note, I mean wings and not spoilers which are incorporated into the bodywork. You can say they bring colour to racing, and I cannot argue against that; but after all F1 racing is meant to be a serious business and not a hot rod show.

2. Wings are dangerous, first to the driver, secondly to the spectators. When wings were first introduced to F1 racing at Spa last year they were tiny spoilers at the front and back of the Ferraris and Brabhams. They had very little effect except at high speed when they were working as a sort of stabiliser. This was a very good effect and nobody thought any more about it until Lotus arrived for the French GP at Rouen a month later with the first proper wing. Suddenly everybody got the message about what could be done with the help of the air; but unfortunately nobody directly concerned gave much thought to what could happen if the wings went wrong, and what effect they would have on racing.

First of all, it is very difficult to design a wing which is going to stand up to all the stresses, because who knows how big the forces are. If you make the wing stronger, it is going to be heavier and therefore produce bigger forces on the construction; you make it lighter and it all goes the opposite way. This is not my wisdom, it all comes from one of the most successful racing car designers. Nevertheless I am sure that after some time – and a few more accidents because of wing failure – this problem could be solved.

Now some personal experience gained by racing with the wing: The wing obviously works via the airflow over it, and this situation changes rapidly if you happen to follow another competitor; he has the full use of the wing and you yourself have to put up with the turbulence created by his car. This could mean that the man in front is actually going slower than you, but you cannot pass him because, after getting near to him, your wings stop working and you cannot go so quickly. This fact spoils racing to quite a large extent. On the other hand the turbulence can be so great that your car starts behaving very strangely and completely unpredictably.

This, I think, explains Oliver's accident at Rouen last year, and I personally have been in similar trouble very often, but luckily I have always managed so far. You will understand that these two facts stop close racing, which is one of the most exciting things to watch. Therefore it is in the interest of the spectators and the drivers to ban wings.

Let us have a look at the wing if something goes wrong with it. And they do go wrong quite often, but so far nobody has been severely hurt. My accident in the Spanish GP has been the biggest one so far and, through a lot of luck and the safety precautions taken by the Spanish organisers, nothing serious happened. Naturally I will always be grateful to the Automobile Club of Barcelona for lining the circuit with double guardrails and for providing such efficient marshals.

To explain the reason for my accident, I was happily driving round the fastest bend on the track when my wing broke and changed its downthrust into reverse. The back end of my car started flying, and I nearly flew over the double guardrail on the left side of the track. Fortunately I was flying about 10 inches too low and got bounced back into the road. I have got a picture to prove it. Can you imagine what would have happened if the car had flown into the crowd? By next year we will probably have wings big enough to do so, and all the owners of the circuits will have to think about new crowd protection. You can also get lift instead of down-pressure if you spin the car at high enough speed and start going backwards.

Altogether I have come to the conclusion that wings are very dangerous, and should therefore be banned.

Jochen Rindt
Begnins, Switzerland

and the CSI soon formally ratified new rules which limited the size and height of wings and specified that they must act on the sprung mass of the car instead of directly into the wheel uprights.

After coming so close to winning the World Championship in 1968, Jackie Stewart made a strong start to 1969 with four wins in the first five races – punctuated by what turned out to be Hill's fifth and final Monaco win. Stewart finished second in Germany and won again in Italy, securing the World Championship with three races still to run. DFV-powered cars won every race and took every pole position in 1969. Hill's season would end in prematurely after he crashed heavily in the United States Grand Prix, breaking both legs. Team-mate Rindt won that race, the 25th Grand Prix win for a DFV-engined car.

For 1970, Matra decreed that its own V12 would be the only engine to power Matra chassis. Ken Tyrrell remained loyal to the Cosworth DFV, and with Ford money he bought a pair of Formula 1 cars from the new March company for Jackie Stewart, Johnny Servoz-Gavin and later the rising French star François Cevert. But the customer Marches were only a stop-gap for Tyrrell. Derek Gardner was engaged to design a completely new car, the Tyrrell 001, which would make its debut at the 1970 Canadian Grand Prix. It, too, would use Cosworth DFV power, which detail development work and a 10,000rpm rev limit had now increased to around 430bhp.

By now most of the field was powered by Cosworth. Lotus's novel Type 72 had a wedge shape derived from the turbine-powered Lotus Indy cars, side-mounted radiators, inboard brakes and rising rate torsion bar suspension – but power still came from the DFV engine. Chris Amon and Jo Siffert ran works March-Fords, while Piers Courage did his best with Frank Williams DFV-engined De Tomaso. Brabham had given up on the Repco engine in 1969 and switched to DFV power, and now produced its first monocoque car. 'Black Jack' proved he was still a force in F1 by winning the first round of the 1970 championship in South Africa, ahead of his old team-mate Denny Hulme in a McLaren-Ford. Stewart won in Spain and Rindt won at Monaco, but at Spa Pedro Rodriguez reminded everyone that there were still a few cars on the grid that didn't rely on Cosworth: his V12 BRM won from Chris Amon's March and the V12 Matra of Jean-Pierre Beltoise. It was the first race Cosworth had lost since the French Grand Prix in 1968, 20 races earlier…

ABOVE: Jackie Stewart, winner of that 1969 Race of Champions, is sitting on his Matra's left front Dunlop poised to catch up with the news from Autosport. Note his Buco helmet with full face shield, and Hinchman fireproof overalls: Stewart was one of the first to campaign for safety in Formula 1

RIGHT: Jackie Stewart and Ken Tyrrell unveil the World Champion's car for 1970: a Cosworth-engined March. High wings had now been banned after a series of failures and two spectacular accidents.

Rindt then won four races in succession in the new Lotus, but in the Austrian's home Grand Prix he retired with a seized engine. Jacky Ickx headed Clay Regazzoni in a Ferrari one–two, the Italian team having now switched from a V12 to a 48-valve flat-12 to provide more clearance and thus better airflow around the rear wing. Rumours suggested the flat-12 generated as much as 460bhp, though it couldn't match the mid-range torque of the DFV. Another Italian engine, the Carlo Chiti-designed Alfa Romeo V8 from the Type 33 sports car, powered the McLaren M7D and M14D driven by Andrea de Adamich. The Alfa V8's power output was supposedly a competitive 430bhp but it was heavy and Alfa Romeo's support for it was inconsistent, and in any case the McLaren team was hit hard in mid-summer by the death of Bruce McLaren in a testing accident at Goodwood.

Ferrari's Clay Regazzoni won a hollow victory at the Italian Grand Prix that year, after Rindt was killed in a practice crash. The Austrian had been running his Lotus 72 without a rear wing, and probably crashed due to the combination of cold tyres and an unfamiliar aerodynamic balance on the car. Team Lotus was not at the next race, in Canada, where Ickx headed another Ferrari one–two with the STP March of Chris Amon upholding

At first, Cosworth insisted that DFVs were rebuilt at Northampton, but eventually there were so many F1 cars using these engines that other engine builders were allowed to take over the maintenance of older units. Improvements included a revised ignition pack sited between the intake trumpets, and Keith Duckworth's famous quill-shaft timing gear which smoothed out troublesome torque spikes in the valvegear.

Jochen Rindt had been injured in a crash in Spain after his rear wing failed, and was particularly pleased to see the suspension-mounted aerofoils banned. Here, Rindt's Lotus 49C, on its way to second place in the Race of Champions, shows its regulation low rear wing, steeply angled front wings and a spoiler to kill lift over the nose. By now, the DFV dominates the grids and Cosworth struggles to keep up with demand for engines...

OPPOSITE: *After winning the 1970 British Grand Prix, Jochen Rindt tells Colin Chapman (right) and Lotus mechanic Eddie Dennis how he did it. Rindt won just one more Grand Prix before his death in practice at Monza later that year.*

BELOW *New Zealander Bruce McLaren was killed at Goodwood in 1970, testing a new Can-Am car. His team was devastated, and it would be nearly two years before they won another Grand Prix.*

the Cosworth runners' honour in third. Emerson Fittipaldi won at Watkins Glen, with his new team-mate Reine Wisell third behind Rodriguez in the BRM and Ickx fourth. It was enough to clinch a posthumous World Championship victory for Jochen Rindt, the Austrian's points tally now being unassailable – although Ickx did his best, with a win in the final round of the championship in Mexico.

Cosworth was now concentrating on building DFVs in quantity and dealing with the remaining reliability concerns. Ten DFVs had been completed by the end of 1967, and by the beginning of 1970 that number was up to 57. As with all Cosworth's engines, the DFV was built using standardised pieces: a spare part bought from Cosworth automatically fitted any DFV engine, without requiring time-consuming (and therefore expensive) handwork. Years before, Coventry Climax engines were supposedly built with interchangeable parts, but often needed a lot of work to make things fit – as Duckworth had discovered during his early days tuning Climax FPFs. More recently the downfall of the Gurney-Weslake V12 had been the lack of standardisation, which made rebuilds long-winded and emergency repairs impossible.

Patrick Head, later responsible for a string of DFV-powered Williams cars, spent a summer working for Weslake while he was at university. 'The machine tools the Eagle-Weslake were machined on were not good enough to hold tolerances. Every single engine was a special – they were all bespoke,' Head recalls. 'There used to be a drawing with tolerances on it, and each cylinder block would have a copy of that drawing. The chap making the engine would put a line through the tolerance on the drawing and write down what he'd got, then they'd have to machine other bits to suit. The cylinder heads were designed to go on that particular cylinder block. When an engine blew up, which they did regularly, some of the obvious interchangeable bits would be taken off, then it used to just get put in a corner.'

According to Head, one of Cosworth's great achievements was to build the DFV using standard parts. 'There was always a rumour that there was a room at Cosworth with a load of saws. If they machined some connecting rods and the bores were too big or the centre distances were outside tolerance, they'd get cut through.' Other engine builders with less fastidious methods would rescue out-of-tolerance components, he says, by modifying the engine to suit – to save scrapping those rods, for instance, a modified piston would be machined and they would get built into an engine. With the DFV, the production engineering was tightly controlled. 'You could put any head on any block, any crank in any block,' says Head. 'All of the tolerancing and quality control, and machining of components so they were either in the tolerances on the drawing or they were scrap; that side was sorted out. Keith was very tough, and wouldn't allow concessions. He scrapped anything that was outside the tolerance, so the machine shop responded and started producing much less scrap. It was almost as big an achievement to make literally a production Formula 1 engine out of it, as the design of the engine itself.'

But during 1970 the production of new DFVs was being hampered by a problem with a batch of crankshafts. The first DFV crankshafts were machined from steel billets, but the 'production' specification was for a stronger forged-steel crank which was Nitrided to improve the surface hardness. In 1970, a whole batch of crankshafts was incorrectly machined, cutting through the Nitrided layer and weakening the cranks, which rapidly broke. Finding the cause was relatively simple, but it took three or four months to make a new batch of crankshafts – to replace a batch which had been

RIGHT: *Emerson Fittipaldi on his way to the third of five wins in 1972, in the British Grand Prix at Brands Hatch.*

OPPOSITE: *Fittipaldi's immaculate JPS-Lotus 72 shows off its side radiators and Firestone tyres as 'Emmo' heads out of the Monza pits in 1972. Tyrrell designer Derek Gardner (blue shirt) watches, while behind him François Cevert is ready to step into Tyrrell 002.*

expected to last a whole year. In the meantime Cosworth had to revive old engines and rescue old crankshafts wherever possible. The result was a shortage of engines for the ever-greater number of teams relying on the DFV to power their Formula 1 machinery.

The sheer number of engines in need of rebuild also began to cause problems, because Cosworth insisted that they looked after every DFV in-house. 'At some meetings you would see a team more engrossed in the organisation of getting broken engines back to Northampton than they were in winning the race,' said Denis Jenkinson in *Motor Sport* early in 1971. 'If your engine was not back at Cosworth before the opposition's you stood a good chance of missing the next race. Some of the races to Northampton indulged in by team-managers and mechanics were more inspiring than those being driven by the team drivers on the track.'

Another problem to hit the DFV around this time was well-known right from the start – the potential for timing-gear failures. Cosworth had experienced the problem on well-used test engines before the DFV ever ran in a car, and then in the debut race at Zandvoort Graham Hill's leading Lotus was eliminated with just such a failure. When Jim Clark's winning engine was

stripped after the race, it too was suffering from the same problems. Numerous detail improvements were made in an effort to solve the problem. The bearings in which the gears ran were upgraded, the geometry of the gear teeth was recalculated and tolerances in the gear-cutting process were tightened up to reduce backlash in the geartrain, which Cosworth thought was contributing to the failures. After much testing Duckworth found that the interaction between the cam timing of the two cylinder banks set up a very rapid torque reversal within the camshaft drive geartrains, resulting in very high and rapidly changing loads which were more than the gear teeth could bear. The instantaneous torque on the gears was recorded at more than 300lb ft, considerably more than the engine produced at the flywheel! New cam profiles reduced the maximum torque required to turn the cams, but the problem persisted.

'I often talked to Keith Duckworth about his Cosworth Ford DFVs and their little problems,' recalled Walter Hassan in his book *Climax in Coventry*. 'Keith is a ruthlessly logical individual who would design every component from first principles if he could only find the time, but he is also refreshingly honest about the inevitable problems which turn up and which he may

Stewart led the most laps in 1972, but Fittipaldi won more races and the World Championship. This is Tyrrell 005, which made its debut part-way through that season, on the way to winning at Mosport.

not immediately understand. The vibration problems which led to breakages in 1969 and 1970 nearly drove him scatty, and we had several talks about similar things that had occurred on our own engines.'

Eventually, Duckworth came up with a solution, which was to introduce some 'give' into the geartrain. The second compound gear, which transferred drive left and right to the camshafts, was mounted on 12 tiny quill shafts which could twist slightly to provide some cushioning. The modification was introduced in 1971, and virtually eliminated the timing gear troubles. But Cosworth still had the problem of keeping up with the growing demand for their engines. To take some of the pressure off, they began to relax the rule which said that DFVs had to be sent back to Northampton for repair or rebuild, a rule applied so rigorously that the teams rarely spent much time trying to diagnose faults with DFVs – they simply changed the engine. Now that Cosworth was busy building new engines, the rebuild work for the growing number of engines in circulation was becoming a headache. Outside engine builders were allowed to rebuild 1969 and 1970 engines, while Cosworth looked after the latest 1971 motors themselves. Lotus and Tyrrell engines were maintained by JW Automotive in Slough, who had raced Cosworth DFVs in their Mirage sports cars in 1969 and would soon do so again later in the 1970s. McLaren and Brabham rebuilt their own engines in-house, and used test facilities at Champion in Feltham run by Brian Muir. March engines were supplied by Brian Hart, while Surtees dealt with Race Engine Services and Bill Lacey at Silverstone.

The 1971 season began with another Ferrari win, this time for Mario Andretti. Jackie Stewart won in Spain and Monaco with Derek Gardner's new Tyrrell-Ford 003, then

BELOW: *Henry Ford II presents Keith Duckworth with a trophy to mark the 50th win for the Cosworth DFV engine. It was a remarkable tally, which had taken just six years to achieve.*

Jacky Ickx underlined his 'rainmaster' reputation with a win in the wet at Zandvoort. Stewart replied with wins in France, Britain and Germany. Against the odds the next two races were won by BRM, Jo Siffert winning in Austria and Peter Gethin dashing to the finish line to win a slipstreaming battle at Monza. The Tyrrells of Stewart and Cevert won the final two championship races. Stewart and Tyrrell-Ford comfortably won their respective titles. Lotus tried a turbine-powered car, the 56B, but Colin Chapman reasoned that if it proved successful it would simply be banned, so the high cost of development was simply not justified.

Cosworth engines again ruled in 1972, with only Ferrari and BRM as occasional challengers. Four drivers won the first four races, but in the second half of the season Emerson Fittipaldi and Jackie Stewart disputed the lead, eventually resolved in favour of Fittipaldi who became the youngest World Champion the sport had yet seen. But it was Stewart who had the honour of recording the DFV's 50th Grand Prix win, at Mosport Park in September. The following year it was again Fittipaldi in the JPS Lotus and Stewart in the Elf Tyrrell who were the front runners. Stewart went on to win four races and the championship, Fittipaldi finished second with three wins. Fittipaldi's team-mate Ronnie Peterson won four races and finished third in the Drivers' Championship, at the same time helping Lotus-Ford to retain their constructors' title. At the end of the season Jackie Stewart retired, and Fittipaldi moved from Lotus to McLaren, where he won another World Championship in 1974 driving the Gordon Coppuck-designed, DFV-powered McLaren M23. In August that year Carlos Reutemann raised the DFV's tally to 75 Grand Prix wins and in October his win at Watkins Glen was the 100th F1 race (including non-championship events) won by a DFV-engined car. Ford marked the event with a press release headed 'The most successful racing engine of all time' in which it detailed the DFV's accomplishments.

By then the Cosworth DFV and Hewland gearbox were the standard wear for many an emerging Grand Prix team. Hesketh started out using Marches but then built its own Harvey Postlethwaite-designed machine for 1974. Graham Hill founded his own team in 1973, initially using Lola cars but later branching out with his own designs. Parnelli, Shadow, Penske, Amon, Token, Ensign, Surtees and Williams were just some of the manufacturers who built their own cars around the off-the-shelf competitive power of the DFV. 'Building cars

Cosworth power took Jackie Stewart to three World Championships. Here, his Tyrrell 006 streaks around Zolder on the way to an emphatic win in the Belgian Grand Prix in 1973.

The 1973 Swedish Grand Prix gets under way, with just a lone Ferrari and a trio of BRMs to add variety to an otherwise all-DFV grid. Peterson already has the edge on Cevert, while Fittipaldi has one eye on his mirrors looking for Stewart's Tyrrell. Reutemann's Brabham BT42 and the Yardley McLarens of Hulme and Revson give chase.

TOP: *Peterson and Fittipaldi (almost hidden) circulated nose-to-tail for much of the 1973 Swedish Grand Prix, with Stewart not far behind.*

ABOVE: *Denny Hulme passes Mike Hailwood's troubled Surtees TS14A in the Swedish Grand Prix. When Peterson's luck ran out – again – and one of the Lotus's rear tyres went soft, Hulme came through to win.*

RIGHT: *Peter Revson wins his first Grand Prix, at Silverstone in 1973. Earlier that afternoon the field had been decimated by a pile-up when Jody Scheckter spun his McLaren in the pack coming out of Woodcote Corner.*

BELOW: *After a confusing wet/dry race which included a myriad of pit-stops and a pace-car period, Peter Revson emerged the winner of the 1973 Canadian Grand Prix to give Yardley McLaren three victories in the season.*

in those days wasn't particularly difficult,' remembers Patrick Head. 'We could go along to Cosworth and buy an engine which was as good as the engine in James Hunt's McLaren.' Enzo Ferrari dismissed them all as mere assemblers of other people's bits – whereas Ferrari, of course, built its own chassis, engines and gearboxes. But more often than not in the 1970s, the 'kit cars' finished ahead of the machines from Maranello…

In 1974, though, the scarlet Ferraris renewed their threat to the DFV's dominance. Niki Lauda began his Formula 1 career with a DFV-powered March in 1971, and after two seasons in the works STP March team he moved to Marlboro BRM for 1973. In 1974 he joined the Scuderia, making him possibly the only driver to have had experience of all three of the existing F1 engines – the DFV, the BRM V12 and Ferrari's flat-12. The Lauda/ Ferrari package won three times that year, and led more laps than anyone, although consistent points finishes moved his team-mate Clay Regazzoni into second place in the championship by the end of the season. But it was clear that Lauda and the Ferrari were a new force in F1. Lauda won five times in 1975 to comfortably secure his first World Championship, with reigning champion Emerson Fittipaldi second in the McLaren with two

Once Ronnie Peterson had finally broken his duck with a win in the French Grand Prix, there was no stopping him. At Watkins Glen in 1973, he celebrated his fourth win of the season, which put him third in the Drivers' Championship.

new faces, Carlos Reutemann (Brabham) and James Hunt (Hesketh), third and fourth. At the end of that year motor racing lost one of its finest ambassadors, Graham Hill, when his light aeroplane crashed in fog on approach to the airfield at Elstree. Hill had been flying back from a testing session with members of his Embassy-Hill team – designer Andy Smallman, mechanics Tony Richards and Tony Alcock, team manager Ray Brimble and the promising young driver Tony Brise – all of whom died in the accident.

Already the DFV was entering its 10th season in competition. In that time the price tag of £7,500 in 1967 had risen to more than £9,000 by 1974, and by 1977 it had almost doubled to nearly £15,000. A well-built engine was now delivering around 475bhp, largely thanks to progressive increases in the rev limit as there were no significant changes to the ports, valves or cam profiles. In 1976, a freshly rebuilt Ferrari flat-12 produced 495bhp at 11,800rpm, although the Ferrari engines tended to lose about 20bhp over the course of a Grand Prix distance due to distortion of the cylinder liners and cylinder heads at high temperatures.

New challenges to the DFV's domination seemed to be coming from all directions, not just Ferrari. Now

Alfa Romeo was back, having abandoned its four-cam V8 engine after desultory performances in McLarens and Marches, in favour of a new Carlo Chiti-designed flat-12, the Tipo 115-12. The Embassy-Hill team built an Alfa-engined version of their Formula 1 Lola, but then the deal fell through. Brabham's Bernie Ecclestone did a deal with Autodelta, Alfa Romeo's in-house racing operation, which gave him free supplies of the Alfa engine, no doubt an attractive alternative to paying Cosworth for DFVs. According to Autodelta, the flat-12 produced no less than 520bhp at 12,000rpm, though there was a marked variety between engines – the Alfa engine men nicknamed each engine, and apparently called the least powerful one 'Bernie'. On the debit side, the Alfa engine was as much as 11 inches (280mm) longer than a DFV and three inches (76mm) wider than the already wide Cosworth V8. The external dimensions of individual engines varied, which led to some headaches when it came to installing them in the cars: Brabham mechanics travelled with a collection of spacers and adaptors in case an engine change was needed.

The engine mounting points were in the cylinder heads on either side of the engine, so Brabham designer Gordon Murray provided a pair of 'booms' which extended backwards from the main monocoque to provide engine mounting points. The booms also accommodated an extra 12 gallons (55 litres) of fuel tank capacity, which was necessary because the Alfa flat-12 was thirstier than the DFV. The Tipo 115-12 was also about 88lb (40kg) heavier than the Cosworth engine, and the extra fuel it required could add another 84lb (38kg), making Murray's attractive-looking BT45 potentially a very heavy machine. Reliability was never the Brabham-Alfas' strongpoint, however, and *Motor Sport*'s Denis Jenkinson was moved to suggest that 'we ought to call them Ecclestone-Alfa Romeos, for Jack Brabham would surely never have got himself involved with such a dead-loss engine.'

Another newcomer to the Formula 1 scene in 1976 was the Ligier JS5, designed by ex-Matra engineer Paul Carillo. The Ligier brought back the unique scream of the Matra V12 engine, which had first been heard in Formula 1 back in 1968. Since then the engine had enjoyed considerable success in sports car racing, winning three Le Mans 24-hour races back to back in 1972–73–74 and it had briefly reappeared in Formula 1 in 1975 powering the Shadow DN7 driven by Jean-Pierre Jarier. The Matra's power output was around 480bhp,

Colin Chapman (left) and Keith Duckworth with the 200th DFV engine in 1974. By the mid-1970s, Cosworth had grown in size and relied on F1 for much of its income. The resurgence of Ferrari in 1975 was a worrying time.

but like the Alfa flat-12 it suffered a fuel-consumption penalty in comparison to the efficient DFV. The bulbous Ligier was a conventional machine in most respects, but had a full-width nose which did not allow for aerodynamic adjustments like the separate wings most teams were using. It also had huge air box which was designed to funnel air to the engine, and quickly gave it the nickname 'the Flying Teapot'. It would not be a consistent race contender, but the Ligier would record a handful of podium finishes (in the hands of Jacques Laffite, and not Jean-Pierre Beltoise as originally planned) including second place in Austria. Guy Ligier's all-French team was sponsored by the Gitanes cigarette brand which led to a rumpus about TV coverage in, ironically, France, which had banned cigarette advertising on TV.

Lauda's Ferrari won the Brazilian and South African Grands Prix at the start of the 1976 season, then finished second to team-mate Regazzoni at Long Beach, and second again to James Hunt (who had taken Fittipaldi's place at McLaren) in Spain. Lauda then won twice more, in Belgium and Monte Carlo, before the Cosworth brigade reasserted themselves.

Ken Tyrrell had groomed Jackie Stewart's team-mate François Cevert as his replacement, but when Cevert was killed in a practice crash at Watkins Glen at the end of 1973, Tyrrell was left with competitive cars, but no drivers. For 1974 he had signed up two rising stars: South African Jody Scheckter and Frenchman Patrick Depailler. Scheckter arrived in F1 with a strong performance in a McLaren at Watkins Glen in 1972, then won himself a deal of notoriety with a spin in the middle of the pack at Silverstone the following year which triggered a multi-car shunt. Like Scheckter, Depailler had raced motorcycles in his youth and then switched to cars, and he had made his Formula 1 debut in 1972 – this time with Tyrrell.

Scheckter and Depailler drove the most distinctive car of the 1976 season, the Derek Gardner-designed, six-wheeled Tyrrell P34. With four small front wheels, Gardner's plan was to improve the aerodynamic penetration of the nose and also provide more tyre contact area to improve braking. That may have been the theory, but Jody Scheckter recalls that it didn't work in practice. 'I always felt it wasn't doing what it was designed to do. On an absolutely flat road it braked quite well, but as soon as you had a bump or a lean one of the wheels locked and you had to lift off your brakes anyway, so I think it was worse.' One area where the P34 did score was its forgiving handling: 'It was very controllable

TOP: *World Champion Emerson Fittipaldi moved to McLaren in 1974, winning his home race at Interlagos and the Belgian GP at Nivelles. At Brands Hatch in July, Emerson is on his way to second place behind Jody Scheckter's Tyrrell 007. The Ferraris can do no better than fourth and fifth, but their time will come…*

BOTTOM LEFT: *At Watkins Glen Fittipaldi finished fourth behind Reutemann and Pace in the Brabhams, and Hunt's Hesketh. The highest-placed non-DFV car was Amon's BRM P201 in ninth place.*

BOTTOM RIGHT: *Emerson Fittipaldi appears on the podium at Watkins Glen in 1974, despite finishing fourth. The Brazilian, with then-wife Maria Helena, is celebrating his second World Championship win.*

– you could put it sideways, you could do anything with it,' Scheckter remembers. Scheckter's P34 won the next race, the Swedish Grand Prix at Anderstorp, with Depailler's sister car second and Lauda's ever-present Ferrari third. Depailler finished second again three weeks later at the French Grand Prix, behind Hunt's McLaren, after Lauda's Ferrari engine failed.

At the British Grand Prix the two Ferraris tangled at the first corner – not for the first time – and the race was stopped. Hunt's McLaren had its steering damaged in the melee, and the McLaren driver limped straight back to the pits through the rear entrance at Graham Hill bend. While stewards and teams argued whether Hunt, Laffite and Regazzoni should be allowed to join the restart in their spare cars – and a restless crowd resorted to a slow hand-clap – Hunt's mechanics beavered away on the M23, replacing the broken right front wishbone. The car was repaired in time to restart. Lauda's Ferrari got the best start but Hunt reeled him in and passed the Austrian to win the race on the road, only to be disqualified weeks later. Ferrari protested that after the first start Hunt had retired before the race was stopped and therefore should not have been allowed to participate in the restart. Initially the protest

was rejected, but Ferrari took the matter to the FIA's International Court of Appeal, which upheld the protest. Hunt was disqualified, promoting Lauda to the race win. But by then an even bigger drama had been played out.

Rain delayed the start of the German Grand Prix at the Nürburgring. Both Hunt's pole-sitting McLaren and Lauda's Ferrari, on the right of the front row, made slow starts and Lauda was running eighth on the long first lap. Halfway round, at the tight right-hand Bergwerk Corner, Lauda's Ferrari clipped a kerb and spun, bouncing from one side of the track to the other. One side of the car was totally destroyed, ripping apart the monocoque and the fuel cells, and the Ferrari burst into flames. Guy Edwards' Hesketh squeezed by, but neither Harald Ertl's Hesketh nor Brett Lunger's Surtees could avoid the burning Ferrari. All three drivers, along with Arturo Merzario who was next to arrive, stopped to help free Lauda from the car. Initial reports suggested he had nothing more than a few burns, despite losing his helmet in the crash, but it soon became clear that Ferrari's team leader was fighting for his life.

Inhalation of fuel and fumes from the fire had caused major damage to Lauda's lungs, and for three days he was on the brink of death. He agreed to see a priest,

thinking he would get an inspiring pep talk, only to be given the Last Rites. Remarkably, though, Lauda was back in the cockpit of a 312T just six weeks later, finishing fourth at Monza. Hunt then won two more races, keeping the championship alive to the final round in Japan. Heavy rain marred the start of the race and Lauda withdrew after a couple of laps, while Hunt raced on to secure third place and the world title – by a single point.

That final 1976 race was won from pole position by Mario Andretti in a Lotus 77, perhaps giving *Motor Sport*'s Denis Jenkinson pause for thought: earlier in the year Jenks had said Andretti 'may be a big wheel in USAC and SCCA kiddy-car racing, but he's dead-duck in European-style Grand Prix racing'. Colin Chapman's original concept for the 77 had been a 'fully adjustable' car which could be set up perfectly for every circuit and circumstance. Tony Rudd, who had long since left BRM and joined Lotus, took some of the wind out of Chapman's sails by calculating that it would take 14 months to try every combination of adjustments on the 77, and the idea never really worked. But Lotus was already working on an innovation which would change the face of F1, and would ultimately give the DFV another lease of life.

CHAPTER SIX

TWELVES AND TURBOS: COSWORTH'S COMPETITION

Late in 1975, Colin Chapman prepared a 27-page briefing document for a new Team Lotus research and development group, to be based at Ketteringham Hall near Hethel, under the watchful eye of Tony Rudd. Chapman's brief suggested that the monocoque of a Formula 1 car could be shaped to generate downforce, providing much more downforce and therefore more grip than could be obtained from the relatively small front and rear wings which were then *de rigueur* in Formula 1. Chapman set the new team the task of turning the idea into a practical proposition.

One member of that team was aerodynamicist Peter Wright, who had worked with Tony Rudd at BRM in the late 1960s. There, he had conducted early investigations into 'ground-effect' aerodynamics for Formula 1 cars and now, at Lotus, Rudd and Wright had the chance to put those ideas into effect. Wright began tests on a model Formula 1 car with a slim monocoque and wing section side pods which, at Rudd's suggestion, carried cooling radiators with intakes at the leading edge of the wing like the Mosquito aircraft. Wind tunnel tests were

Andretti put the Lotus 79 on pole for its first race, at Zolder in 1978. Moments after the start Reutemann's Ferrari has its nose in front of the Lotus – but the American is on the inside for turn one. Behind them Niki Lauda holds third, but neither Lauda nor Hunt in the McLaren will finish lap one. Peterson's Lotus 78, starting a lowly seventh on the grid, is heading for second place.

RIGHT: *Mario Andretti's Lotus 78 ushered in a new era of 'ground-effect' aerodynamics. Here, the American hustles through the streets of Long Beach on the way to the 78's first win, in April 1977.*

BELOW: *Walter Wolf took over sole ownership of the Wolf-Williams team for 1977, running a single Wolf WR1 car for Jody Scheckter.*

carried out to prove the concept, and in December 1975 Rudd received a simple message: 'the Mosquito flies'. A new Lotus Formula 1 car, the Type 78, was prepared to these 'wing car' principles, but in the meantime the existing 77s were modified using some of the lessons learned.

During 1977, Mario Andretti and Gunnar Nilsson regularly proved that the Lotus 78 had grip to spare, but there was a price to pay and that was excessive aerodynamic drag. Andretti neatly summed it up by pointing out that, in a straight line, the 78 'couldn't get out of its own way'. Despite that Andretti was well placed in three Grands Prix that season, only to be let down by unreliable 'development' engines from Cosworth – one of those races being at Monaco, where Jody Scheckter came through to win the DFV's 100th Grand Prix victory in the Wolf WR1. Lotus switched to DFVs from Nicholson-McLaren in the search for reliability. Although Andretti won four times that year, Niki Lauda exploited the Ferrari 312T's 500bhp and its exceptional reliability to win a second World Championship. But the most intriguing new car of the season boasted even more power than the Ferrari – despite having half the capacity and half the number of cylinders.

Renault's first foray into Formula 1 came at the British Grand Prix at Silverstone in 1977, with a car which had already been under development for a year. The yellow and black Renault RS01 was the first example of a Formula 1 car built to the '1.5-litres supercharged' regulations which had existed alongside the '3.0-litres unsupercharged' regulations since the start of the formula in 1966. Renault, however, was employing a different method of forced induction to that envisaged when the regulations were written. Instead of using a supercharger, an engine-driven pump pushing air into the intake, the Renault engine was fitted with a turbocharger. A turbine driven by engine exhaust gases was connected to a compressor which pressurised the intake air, converting 'lost' energy in the exhaust gases into useful work. Renault had already proved the technology in its 2.0-litre turbocharged sports cars, which had won at Mugello in 1975 and had recorded fastest laps at Monza and Watkins Glen.

The Renault-Gordini engine was a compact 90-degree V6 with four valves per cylinder operated by twin overhead camshafts on each bank of cylinders. For Formula 1 it was reduced in capacity to 1,492cc, and featured a very short stroke. Compressed air from the single Garrett AiResearch turbocharger, mounted over the gearbox, was supplied to the engine through an intercooler to reduce charge temperatures and maximise volumetric efficiency. The rest of the car was a conventional monocoque design, and like the Ligier, it quickly substituted a full-width fairing nose for a more adaptable chisel-nose with separate wings. The engine was certainly powerful – over 500bhp was available, depending on the boost pressure employed – but at first it lacked reliability. The lone Renault of Jean-Pierre Jabouille did not finish a race in 1977.

Although there were now more challengers to the DFV's dominance and they were steadily improving, most of the teams in F1 that year stuck with the tried and tested DFV. 'At the British Grand Prix, there were so many teams wanting to enter that there was a pre-qualifying day on the Wednesday – the first time Gilles Villeneuve drove a McLaren,' remembers Patrick Head of Williams. 'There were 26 starters in the Grand Prix and about 40 entries. We had to battle it out with the other teams to get into qualifying. All these cars would have had DFV engines. The DFV made F1 accessible, where it hadn't really been accessible before. Installing a V12 Maserati engine, or something, was not easy.' By

LEFT: *Scheckter won the first Grand Prix of 1977, in Argentina, then clocked up the DFV's 100th Grand Prix victory in Monte Carlo.*

BELOW: *Jody Scheckter has the Monaco Grand Prix trophy just about under control, watched by Prince Rainier of Monaco.*

RIGHT: *Renault's turbocharged RS01 appeared in 1977. At first it was unreliable, but the French team gradually developed the turbocharged V6 into a potential race-winner.*

OPPOSITE: *Mario Andretti at the wheel of the car which took him to the World Championship in 1978, the Lotus 79. Venturi tunnels under the car created downforce which improved the car's cornering ability. Suddenly a V-shaped engine was almost essential, giving the DFV a new lease of life.*

contrast, says Head, the DFV was relatively simple to plumb into a car. 'Keith Duckworth always had a healthy contempt for car designers. With the DFV you got a very simple installation document – basically they told you exactly what pipe sizes to use, all the information, and as long as you followed that information, generally you would have a reliable engine. The one area that wasn't that competent to begin with was the Lucas Opus ignition system. The rev limiter really wasn't that competent. If you buzzed the engine, missed a gear, it would allow the engine to over-rev.'

In 1978, Lotus took the 'wing car' concept a stage further with the Type 79, which had venturi-shaped tunnels hidden in its side pods to generate downforce through 'ground-effect'. Air entering at the front of the side pod was squeezed through a progressively smaller area between the side pod and the road surface, causing the air to accelerate and its pressure to fall. It was the same principle that was used in the venturi of a carburettor, only here the low-pressure area that was created sucked the car down onto the road. Careful management of the under-car airflow was critical to making the system work. Flexible plastic skirts were fitted to the outer edges of the side pods to seal the

gap to the road, preventing air at ambient pressure rushing into the low-pressure area. The Type 78's side-mounted fuel tanks were replaced by a larger, single tank directly behind the driver, which meant moving the driving position further forward. The rear suspension springs were inboard, and new exhaust manifolds swept upwards out of the air flow. The DFV contributed enormously to the package: its compact size and narrow-bottomed shape were ideal for minimising the disturbance to the under-car airflow. Flat engines, like those used by Ferrari and Alfa Romeo, were at a distinct disadvantage.

Lotus continued to run their 78s until the non-championship International Trophy at Silverstone in March, where Andretti gave the 79 its race debut – retiring with a gearbox failure. Andretti put the 79 on pole position at Zolder in May and ran away with the race, with team-mate Ronnie Peterson finishing second in his 78. Andretti put the 79 on pole again at Jarama two weeks later, again won the race and recorded the fastest lap for good measure. Peterson now had a 79 too, and finished second behind his team leader. The aerodynamic development of the Lotus 79 had clearly put it in a different class to everything else – until the

RUNNING REPAIRS: DFV MAINTENANCE

When the DFV was in front-line service in F1, the top teams generally ran individual engines for about 500 miles between rebuilds. The night before a race a fresh engine would be installed, and it would hopefully complete Sunday morning warm-up, the race, and then the qualifying sessions at the next Grand Prix weekend. The engine would then be sent to an engine builder or back to Cosworth for a rebuild.

At Northampton a day's work went into stripping each engine. Pistons, valve springs and oil pump internals were routinely replaced at each rebuild, along with the big-end bolts if the engine had been over-revved, and other components were inspected and crack-tested to avoid failures in service. Coils were changed every 12 months, and in the interim the ignition pack was tested on a complex device suitable nicknamed the 'Heath Robinson Memorial'.

Dynamometer tests followed the rebuild, and the final job was an inspection – including an endoscope check of the combustion chambers to look for damage caused during the dyno run. The whole rebuild took 120 hours and cost around £5,000 in early-1980s money – then the price of a new Ford Escort. And that was for an engine with no significant problems, simply needing a regular service – but the result was an engine ready for 500 miles at the very top of international motor sport.

qualified second and third on the grid at Anderstorp, splitting the two Lotuses. Arguments raged over the legality of the Brabhams: if the fans were there primarily to provide aerodynamic downforce they were clearly illegal, under the rule which stated that any aerodynamic component must be immovably attached to the car. The rotating fan clearly wasn't immovable. Further objections came from the drivers of cars that had followed close behind the Brabhams in practice, who complained that the rear-mounted fan sucked up any on-track debris and flung it at the car behind. Despite all the protests the 'fan car' was allowed to race and Lauda recorded an untroubled win. Riccardo Patrese finished second in the new Arrows A1, a Tony Southgate-designed Cosworth/Hewland 'kit car'.

A week later the 'fan car' was officially banned, though oddly Lauda's Swedish Grand Prix victory was allowed to stand. The teams then went to Paul Ricard for the French Grand Prix, where the Brabhams reverted to a no-fan design and still proved to be quick in practice, Watson claiming the outside of the front row just a few hundredths behind Andretti's Lotus 79. Watson got away from the start better than Andretti but the lead lasted less than a lap, leaving the American to win the race with Peterson close behind in second. Watson finished fourth behind Hunt's McLaren, Lauda's Alfa Romeo engine having let go early on.

Peterson won pole position at Brands Hatch two weeks later, with Andretti beside him on the front row and Lauda sharing the second row with Jody Scheckter's Wolf, Patrese's Arrows fifth and Alan Jones sixth in the Williams. Of the top six qualifiers only Lauda survived to the end, finishing second behind Reutemann's Ferrari with his Brabham-Alfa team-mate John Watson third. Peterson's fuel pump had failed, Andretti's engine had let go, Scheckter had gearbox trouble, Patrese suffered a suspension failure and Jones broke a driveshaft. Watson and Patrick Depailler in the Tyrrell came from the middle of the grid to finish third and fourth respectively. Hockenheim proved a happier race for the Cosworth-engined teams, Andretti winning from pole from Scheckter's Wolf. Peterson won in Austria, then Andretti took a third successive victory for the Lotus 79 at the Dutch Grand Prix, with Peterson second. But tragedy struck at Monza.

Andretti put his Lotus 79 on pole, but Peterson's 79 suffered an engine failure in practice and he reverted to his spare car, a 78, which he qualified fifth. The start was a shambles, as so often at Monza; the green light

TOP: *Andretti's Lotus 79 shows off its full-length venturi-profile side pods during the Belgian Grand Prix. The 79 revolutionised F1 aerodynamics.*

ABOVE: *Lotus had two 79s for the Spanish Grand Prix in 1978. This is Andretti on the way to winning his second race in succession.*

teams got to Anderstorp for the Swedish Grand Prix, where a new challenger appeared for the first time.

Brabham's Gordon Murray adopted a very different method of creating a low-pressure area under the car for his new Brabham BT46B. Like Jim Hall's Chaparral 2H Can-Am car of 1970, the BT46B used a fan to suck the air from under the car. On the Chaparral there were two fans driven by a Snowmobile engine, but the Brabham had a single fan driven from the engine and claimed to be primarily for cooling. Quite why the BT46B needed a vast fan to cool it when the same car with the same Alfa engine had previously managed quite happily without one was not explained. Clearly the aerodynamic advantages were real, as John Watson and Niki Lauda

was given before the back half of the grid had rolled to a stop, giving slower cars at the back an advantage over the quicker cars at the front. As the tightly packed field funnelled into the narrower section of track beyond the pits, Hunt's McLaren was nudged into Peterson's Lotus and the Swede's 78 veered off to the right into a crash barrier before bursting into flames. In the ensuing pile-up Brambilla's Surtees lost a wheel, which clouted the driver on the helmet and knocked him out. Hunt and Regazzoni dragged Peterson from the burning Lotus, and he was despatched to hospital with badly broken legs. The Brabham-Alfas of Lauda and Watson finished first and second in the restarted race after Andretti and Villeneuve were docked a minute for jumping the start, but Andretti won a point for sixth place and secured the 1978 Drivers' Championship in the process. After lengthy surgery to set his shattered legs, Peterson was expected to make a full recovery, but complications arose during the night. The following morning his fellow drivers and many fans woke to the grim news that 'SuperSwede' was dead.

Andretti secured pole at Watkins Glen a full second in front of Reutemann's Ferrari, but his race car lost a wheel in the Sunday warm-up session and he was

forced to race the T-car. With a guessed set-up Andretti was plagued with poor handling and finally suffered an engine failure, leaving Reutemann to secure a convincing win in the flat-12 Ferrari. In Canada, pole went to Jean-Pierre Jarier, who had been drafted in to drive the second Lotus, and the Frenchman built up a huge lead before retiring with brake troubles. Ferrari won again, but this time it was Villeneuve in the winning car – his first Grand Prix victory.

For 1979, Villeneuve was joined at Ferrari by a new team-mate. Jody Scheckter had decided to leave Wolf, though the team had been keen to keep him, and had suggested to him that the DFVs the team were using would soon have the power to match the Ferraris. 'They were bringing bits and pieces out all the time,' Scheckter says. 'When I was leaving Wolf to go to Ferrari, I had a long conversation with Keith Duckworth – they were coming out with something very special, that was going to beat everything. But I don't remember anything ever coming out…'

So Scheckter moved to the Maranello team. It was a successful season which ended up with the South African as World Champion, but he was surprised to find that the Ferrari flat-12 was not significantly more powerful

The popular Ronnie Peterson broke both legs in a crash at the start of the Italian Grand Prix in 1978. His injuries did not seem life-threatening, but sadly he died due to complications after surgery.

than the DFV he was used to. 'They always had a massive pride in the 12-cylinder engine,' he remembers. 'After I'd done Brazil in the Ferrari, we had a debriefing with all the people at Ferrari – there was Forghieri, the Old Man, Piero Lardi. I said the Ferrari was slower than the Cosworth, and they didn't translate. So I said it again – tell him that the power was less. He didn't translate. They wouldn't tell him, because they knew there would be such bloodshed… I communicated directly with him [Enzo Ferrari] after that, I used to send him a fax and that was translated and given to him directly.'

Ferrari's flat-12 engine prevented them from building a true ground-effect car like the Lotus 79, because the horizontal cylinder banks got in the way of the airflow under the car. More compact cylinder heads and repositioned exhaust manifolds helped, and at one stage there was even talk of rotating the flat-12 through 90 degrees about its crankshaft centreline to produce a tall, narrow engine with plenty of space either side for ground-effect tunnels – though, perhaps mercifully, that was never pursued. At Brabham Gordon Murray was suffering the same problems with the Alfa flat-12, and began scheming the BT47, a complex ground-effect car which seated the driver as far forward as possible with the Alfa flat-12 engine right behind him. A propeller shaft connected the engine to the gearbox/final drive unit. Fuel tanks were carried behind the engine, and shaped to provide the 'venturi' underside essential to create downforce through ground-effect. Then Alfa Romeo moved the goalposts by building a V12 engine, in just four months, and Murray drew up the BT48 ground-effect car to use it. Performance variation between engines proved to be a major headache, as Murray later told *Motor Sport* magazine: 'The Alfa Romeo V12s varied alarmingly – as much as 600rpm at full song – from engine to engine. Eventually we found out that the real problem was Alfa Romeo's oil scavenging system. Some worked, others simply drowned the crankcase.'

Williams was fast emerging as one of the most competitive teams in Formula 1, with cars designed by Patrick Head and driven in 1979 by Alan Jones and Clay Regazzoni. Head came up with the ground-effect FW07, which developed the principles first seen on the Lotus 79 more effectively than any other F1 machine of the time (including Chapman's troublesome Lotus 80). 'The DFV was well-suited to a ground-effect car,' says Head, pointing out that the only drawback was the arrangement of some of the ancillaries along the sides of the engine. 'When the FW07 first ran it had the

Emerging rivals for the Cosworth DFV's domination in 1979: Jean-Pierre Jabouille's Renault RS10 and Gilles Villeneuve's oversteering Ferrari 312T4.

standard water pump on, which stuck out wider than the chassis and was interrupting the air flow under the car. For the British Grand Prix we actually modified the water pump housing – we cut off the inlet for it and welded on our own inlet pipe which was much tighter in, which allowed us to panel in the side of the chassis and gave us a lot more downforce. It was almost worth a second a lap, the kind of development we'd love to have now.' Unfortunately the early versions of the modified housing were, says Head, 'over-fettled' inside and Jones retired with a water leak – but Regazzoni won. 'We went about modifying them rather better from then on, but then Cosworth modified their casting and we were able to use that.' Cosworth could still recognise a good idea, although as Head says, 'Keith was quite contemptuous about chassis people fiddling with his engine.'

The last race of 1979 was at Watkins Glen, where Williams feared engine problems. The day before the race Frank Williams received an anguished phone call from Cosworth explaining that a rogue batch of valve springs had ended up in some recently rebuilt DFVs – but there was no way of knowing exactly which engines they were in. 'I'm a Roman Catholic, a bad one,' says Williams. 'I thought about it a great deal, and

Jody Scheckter moved from Wolf to Ferrari for 1979, expecting the flat-12 engine to be much more powerful than the Cosworth DFV – but it didn't work out that way...

Renault won its first Grand Prix in France in 1979, finally proving that the powerful turbo engines could be made reliable enough to complete a race distance.

I thought the best thing I could do was go to Watkins Glen and have a Roman Catholic mass at six o'clock in the morning. So I went up there, did my duty and came back with a smug smile on my face.' Wet weather at the start persuaded most of the field to start on wet tyres, and Villeneuve's Michelin-shod Ferrari led from Jones's Williams, running on Goodyears. On the very wet track Villeneuve built up a comfortable lead, but then the rain eased off allowing Jones to catch and pass the Ferrari. With the track drying out both drivers had to stop for slick tyres. 'Alan lasted about three quarters of a lap before a wheel came off,' remembers Williams. 'I'd prayed for the valve springs, but I forgot to pray for the wheel changes…'

Brabham abandoned Alfa Romeo engines late in 1979 and returned to the DFV. Another team to adopt the Cosworth V8 was Ligier, now running two cars, for Jacques Laffite and Patrick Depailler. The other French team, Renault, also ran two cars with René Arnoux joining Jean-Pierre Jabouille. Although it would be Ferrari's season, Laffite and Depailler would both win races for Ligier-Ford and Jabouille would win in France, where Villeneuve won a spectacular duel with Arnoux for second place.

Williams was clearly the class of the field in 1980, with Alan Jones winning in Argentina, France, Britain, Canada and Watkins Glen to wrap up the Drivers' Championship. Frank Williams particularly remembers beating Pironi and Laffite in the Ligiers on home ground. 'It was Alan at his best. Every lap at the end of the straight, with a bit of a tail wind, the engine was revving at 10,900rpm or 11,100rpm. There was no way it would last, but it did and it won. And we stuffed the French!'

Nelson Piquet was runner-up in the Drivers' Championship that year in Gordon Murray's new Cosworth-engined Brabham BT49, at first using a standard Hewland gearbox, but later revised with a narrow Weismann gearbox to improve under-car airflow and add downforce. Carlos Reutemann was third in his first season for Williams, helping the team to win its first constructors' title. Reutemann, incidentally, was very superstitious. 'He always had a favourite engine – 312, I think it was. He always wanted to have the same engine all the time,' remembers Patrick Head. Clive Chapman recalls that Team Lotus drivers had a similar fascination. 'Drivers used to get attached to engines. They'd always want to know what the engine number was. It was the first question they'd ask,' he says. Testing logs kept by engineer Steve Hallam, and now part of the Classic Team Lotus archive, reveal that a particular engine praised by one driver was sometimes condemned by another...

Renault had won another three races, proving that the

ABOVE: *The 1979 championship-winning Ferrari 312T4, in Jody Scheckter's private museum of racing cars. Although lacking the ground-effect capabilities of other cars on the grid, the Ferrari was an effective package and a consistent race winner.*

LEFT: *Jabouille celebrates his, and Renault's first Grand Prix win, on the podium at Dijon, flanked by team-mate Rene Arnoux (left) and Ferrari's Gilles Villeneuve.*

ABOVE: *Patrick Head's Williams FW07 chassis and the ever-present Cosworth DFV V8 provided Alan Jones with a fast and reliable package for 1980. The Australian won five times that year on the way to the World Championship.*

RIGHT: *Jones made the best possible start to the 1980 season with a win from pole position in the first race, in Argentina.*

LEFT: *The FW07 developed the 'ground-effect' principles introduced by the Lotus 79. While Lotus struggled to refine their original concept, the Williams proved very successful.*

BELOW: *Jones and the Williams FW07 on their way to first place in Canada, 1980, with team-mate Reutemann second. Williams used DFVs with 'Cosworth' cam covers rather than 'Ford' ones, in deference to their sponsor Leyland Trucks!*

ABOVE: *The combination of Brazilian driver Nelson Piquet and the Cosworth-engined Brabham BT49C designed by Gordon Murray was competitive right from the start of the 1981 season. Piquet's first win of the year came in Argentina.*

RIGHT: *Piquet won the World Championship for the first time in 1981, but Brabham lost the Constructors' Championship to Williams. Piquet's team-mate Hector Rebaque suffered poor reliability, and failed to qualify in Monaco.*

Renault signed up Alain Prost to partner René Arnoux in 1981, and 'The Professor' rewarded them with three Grand Prix victories that season. This is the third of them, at Monza, where the Williams FW07s of Jones and Reutemann were second and third.

BMW entered Formula 1 in 1982, supplying this turbocharged in-line four to Brabham for Nelson Piquet and Riccardo Patrese. BMW joined Renault, Ferrari and the Hart-powered Tolemans in the turbo ranks – but the DFV still did the lion's share of the winning that year.

reliability problems which had plagued them were slowly being overcome. Now in twin-turbo form, the 1.5-litre V6 was developing more power than ever, and Renault was no longer the only team to think turbo engines were worthy of development. Gordon Murray was working on the Brabham BT50, to be powered by a four-cylinder BMW turbo engine, while Ferrari was developing a 1.5-litre V6 turbo to power its new 126C. Another new turbo engine to appear in 1981 came from Brian Hart. Based on Hart's four-cylinder 420R Formula 2 engine, it would soon be seen in the new Toleman cars.

The turbo engines were now producing well over 600bhp, far more than the Cosworth DFV – though the Cosworth engine was, at least, consistent. 'Inevitably you'd have the odd 10bhp difference, but within the limits of what actually made a difference, they were all the same,' says Patrick Head. 'When we were severely challenged by the Renault engine getting more and more powerful each year we realised we were going to have difficulties keeping competitive with the DFV turning up at 475bhp every year, so we went up for a meeting with Keith Duckworth to try and persuade him to do some more development on the engine. He was not particularly responsive, so we went off and did a deal

Paul Rosche was the man behind the BMW turbo engine, eventually marshalling its development so effectively that test engines produced more power than BMW's dynamometer was capable of measuring!

ABOVE: *Brabham ran BMW-engined and DFV-engined cars throughout 1982. At Monaco, Piquet's BMW-engined BT50 broke its gearbox. Despite a spin in the closing stages, team-mate Patrese's Cosworth-engined BT49C won the race.*

RIGHT: *Keke Rosberg emerged as World Champion for Williams after a scrappy 1982 season which saw no less than 11 different drivers win races. At Zandvoort the Finn finished third behind Piquet's Brabham-BMW and Pironi's Ferrari, just a second ahead of Lauda's McLaren.*

124 FORD COSWORTH DFV

ABOVE: *Turbo cars dominated the front end of the grid at the Austrian Grand Prix in 1982, with the Brabhams on the front row and Prost's Renault sharing the second row with Tambay's Ferrari. Rosberg was the quickest of the Cosworth contingent, lining up in sixth place alongside Arnoux's Renault. It was Patrese who would lead in the early stages, but the turbo challenge soon faded...*

LEFT: *In Austria, the BMW and Renault engines failed and Tambay's Ferrari lost time with a puncture. Elio de Angelis inherited the lead in his Lotus 91 and despite a late charge from Rosberg he held on to win his first Grand Prix. It was the first Lotus win since 1978, the 150th win for the DFV – and the last time Colin Chapman would see his cars win a race.*

with John Judd, and we developed the DFVs.'

Part of that development sought to raise the safe rev limit for the engine, in the search of more power. 'Patrick has a great friend called Chris Walters, who is a very clever mathematician – which means I hold him in awe,' says Frank Williams. 'He came up with the calculations which allowed the engine to rev higher, and we put slightly more aggressive camshafts in it.' The DFV's weakness was its valve train, something which Cosworth had attempted to address by designing desmodromic valve gear – a system which positively closed the valves rather than relying on a valve spring. But Duckworth decided it would be very difficult to make a reliable system, and he cancelled the project.

But the DFV family was not entirely without development in what would prove to be the final years of its career as a 3.0-litre Formula 1 engine. Cosworth engineer Mario Ilien reworked the DFV with a larger bore and shorter stroke, and as a further evolution drew up a new cylinder head with an even narrower valve angle, just 16 degrees, and fitted new camshafts. The result was the DFY, with more top-end power than the DFV and also a useful reduction in weight, of about 44lb (20kg). According to Patrick Head the best of the DFYs

ABOVE: *Alfa Romeo introduced a turbo V8 in 1982 to replace its 3.0-litre V12. For 1983 former European F3 Champion Mauro Baldi joined the team.*

RIGHT: *Brabham re-introduced planned pit-stops to Formula 1 in 1982, and in 1983 all the teams adopted the strategy of running a low fuel load and softer, grippier tyres with a mid-race stop for fresh rubber and more fuel. Fuel stops minimised the penalty of the turbo engine's higher fuel consumption, and soon became an integral part of a Grand Prix afternoon.*

produced near enough the same output as Williams's own Judd-developed DFVs. 'I think the best we had on Judd's dyno was about 540bhp which we raced in 1982 with Keke Rosberg.' says Head. 'We never had to buy any DFYs because we had our own development programme.'

Williams won the Constructors' Championship again in 1981 in what proved to be a wide-open season: eventual Drivers' Champion Piquet and new Renault signing Alain Prost won three races each, Reutemann, Jones, Laffite and Villeneuve won two each, and John Watson delivered a very popular home win in the British Grand Prix, driving for McLaren. The main opposition to the DFV continued to be the Ferrari flat-12 and the turbo Renault, though an old campaigner was back in the game at Ligier. The French team's new sponsors, Talbot, had very nearly pulled off a coup by taking over BMW's turbo four when it was still under development, but that deal had been quashed at the last moment. Now they objected to Ligier's use of the Cosworth-Ford V8, and Ligier was forced to revert back to the old Matra V12.

In 1982, the reigning champion would swap back and forth between the Cosworth-powered Brabham BT49C and BT49D and the BMW turbo-engined BT50 – failing

Gordon Murray's Brabham-BT52, with BMW turbo power. New regulations for 1983 banned ground-effect aerodynamics and sliding skirts

to qualify the BT50 in Detroit but then winning with it in Canada a week later! From then on Piquet stuck with the Brabham-BMW, finishing second at Zandvoort and fourth at Dijon. Renault seemed to have their reliability problems finally ironed out, Prost and Arnoux winning two races apiece. Ferrari, too, was getting to grips with its turbo car, but practice accidents which killed Gilles Villeneuve and severely injured Didier Pironi were huge setbacks for the Maranello team.

Despite the turbo-powered opposition, the Cosworth-engined cars still put in some good performances. Reutemann's Williams split the Renaults in South Africa, Piquet won in Brazil in the Cosworth-engined Brabham, Lauda won at Long Beach in the McLaren, and his team-mate John Watson won at Zolder. Monaco saw a bizarre race. Rain fell a few laps from the end and leader Alain Prost crashed at the chicane, letting Patrese into the lead. Patrese spun at the Loews hairpin and almost blocked the road, so the marshals pushed him out of the way and the Italian managed to bump-start the DFV as the Brabham rolled downhill. Meantime Pironi had inherited the lead, but his Ferrari expired in the tunnel. Now Andrea de Cesaris was leading – but his Alfa ran out of fuel. Patrese finally emerged the winner, though even he didn't realise it at the time...

Cosworth-engined McLarens won in Detroit and Britain, and then Elio de Angelis won the DFV's 150th victory at the Österreichring in Austria, less than a car's length ahead of a charging Keke Rosberg. It was the last time Colin Chapman would see one of his cars win: he died that December, aged just 54. Rosberg won the next race, at Dijon. The final race of the season, in Las Vegas, was another victory for the DFV, this time powering Michele Alboreto's Tyrrell. Rosberg emerged from scrappy season as World Champion, with Ferrari taking the constructors' title.

One of the most remarkable Cosworth wins of all was chalked up early in 1983 at Long Beach, by John Watson. 'Wattie' qualified a lowly 22nd in his DFV-engined McLaren MP4/1C, but fought through the field to take the victory, aided by a string of retirements – while his team-mate Niki Lauda, who qualified 23rd, finished second! Keke Rosberg demonstrated the biggest advantage of the normally aspirated Cosworth engine, its instant and precise throttle response, with a win at Monaco. 'In the early days of the turbos they had very poor throttle response, so when you went to a track like Monaco they were very difficult to drive,' says Patrick Head. A few weeks later, Alboreto's DFY-engined Tyrrell

OPPOSITE: *Piquet won three races in 1983 to Alain Prost's four, but the Brazilian took the world title by just two points. Arnoux and Tambay finished third and fourth in the championship, accumulating enough points between them to win the constructors' title for Ferrari. Williams was the highest-placed non-turbo team, in fourth, and the writing was on the wall for the DFV.*

ABOVE LEFT: *Nelson Piquet's first World Championship came in 1981 in a Brabham-Cosworth. His second, in 1983, was won in a Brabham-BMW.*

LEFT: *The definitive DFY was a short-stroke, big-bore version of the DFV with even narrower valve angles inside revised cylinder heads, drawn up by Mario Ilien. Ilien and fellow Cosworth engineer Paul Morgan later founded the Ilmor company.*

ABOVE: *Michele Alboreto's Tyrrell 011 shows off its short-stroke Cosworth DFY engine at the Detroit Grand Prix in 1983. Alboreto won the race, the 155th and final victory for the DFV family in Formula 1.*

OPPOSITE: *Tyrrell continued to use DFV engines throughout 1983 and into 1984, but the non-turbo cars were increasingly outclassed. This is Alboreto at Silverstone, a power circuit, where he could qualify no better than 16th and finished 13th.*

won at Detroit – another tight and twisty street circuit. It was to be the 155th and last outright victory for the Cosworth DFV series of engines in Formula 1.

In 1984, only cash-strapped Tyrrell had normally aspirated engines: every other team had turbo power. The new Williams FW09 had a Honda V6 turbo, which Patrick Head recalls had masses of power but a distinctly on/off delivery. 'It had a 6.5:1 compression ratio, and great long exhaust pipes up to the turbo – when it was off boost it was like a shopping engine, it was terrible, but then it came in with a bang about two seconds after you put your foot on the throttle. Later on they sorted that out and you had response almost as good as a normally aspirated engine, and an extra 150bhp. There was nothing you could do to compete – you had to go with a turbo.'

Soon Formula 1 would be entirely populated by turbocharged engines, and the beginning of the high-boost era and qualifying engines with well over 1,000bhp was about to begin. But, remarkably, it was not the end of the road for the Cosworth DFV family. The most successful F1 engine of all had already diversified into other areas of motorsport, and in just a few years it would be back at the heart of Formula 1.

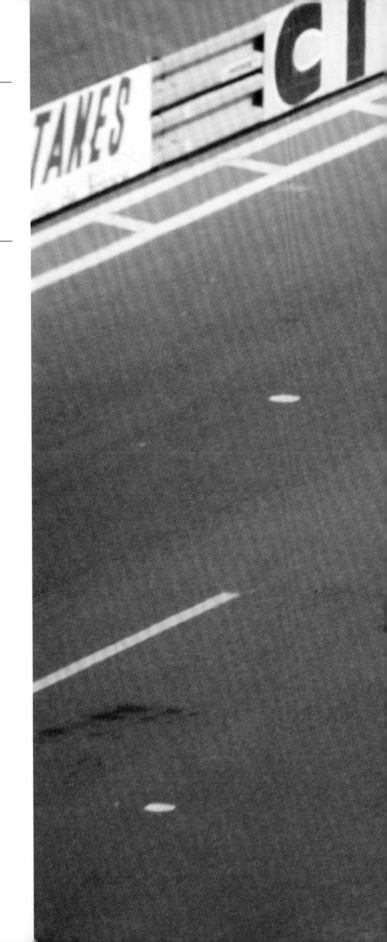

CHAPTER SEVEN

ENDURING ACHIEVEMENTS

America has always had its own classes of motorsport, its own sets of racing rules and regulations and its own, unique, venues. Indianapolis, Daytona and Sebring were the centre of motorsport as far as Americans were concerned in the 1960s. Men like Foyt, Unser, Gurney and Shelby were the all-American heroes of 'auto racing'. Yes, the Europeans had arrived with their 'funny cars' to revolutionise Indy, so Americans had heard of Cooper and Lotus, and Brabham, Clark and Hill. And everyone, even on the far side of the Atlantic, had heard of Ferrari. Now there was even a United States Grand Prix, at Watkins Glen, that was starting to introduce Americans to Formula 1. But for most Americans there were only two European events of note – the Monaco Grand Prix, and the greatest of all the sports car races, the Le Mans 24-hours. It was the latter which Ford set out to win in the 1960s.

Ford's 'Total Performance' image extended as far as negotiating to buy Ferrari in 1963, a plan which was intended to create two new companies. Ford-Ferrari was to be controlled by Ford, and would build high-profile, high-performance road cars using Ferrari know-how. Ferrari-Ford would be controlled by Enzo Ferrari, and would look after Ferrari's sports car and Formula 1 racing activities. Negotiations progressed a long way before Ferrari backed out, no doubt realising that Ford did not intend to simply invest in his company and then leave him alone to run it. Ultimately, Ferrari would be bought by Fiat, which would bankroll the racing activities

The Gulf GR8 of Jacky Ickx and Derek Bell, with the Briton driving, heads for victory in the Le Mans 24-hour race in 1975. It was the first Le Mans win for the Cosworth DFV, and the first of many wins as a team for these two experienced sports car drivers.

as a matter of Italian pride. Ford's response to the breakdown of negotiations was simple: if you can't join 'em, beat 'em. Ford would take on Ferrari in endurance sports car racing, an arena where the Italian team was almost unchallenged, and would win. That meant producing a sports-racing car to beat Ferrari at Le Mans.

The result was the GT40, based on Eric Broadley's Lola GT concept and built by a new organisation, Ford Advanced Vehicles, in Slough, Berkshire. The Lola had been fitted with a 260ci US Ford V8, driving the rear wheels through a four-speed Colotti transaxle, and though its first two races in 1963 were unsuccessful the concept clearly had potential. Through 1963 and the spring of 1964 Lola expertise was put to work on the new Ford, which was given a pressed and folded sheet-steel monocoque with unstressed outer panels in glassfibre. The most recognisable feature was the door shape, which cut heavily into the roof to allow easy entry and exit despite the overall height of 40in (1,016mm) which gave the car its name. Aerodynamic problems afflicted early GT40s, and the cars were not nearly as fast as Ford's computers had predicted. But painstaking development paid off, and the GT40 was turned into a

race-winner. The addition of 7.0-litre V8 engines, a spin-off from Ford's NASCAR Galaxie programme, proved to be the turning point. In 1966, Henry Ford II was at Le Mans to see the achievement he had been waiting for, the big Fords finishing first, second and third in the French classic. Ford ended its involvement in sports car racing, its point made. At the end of the year, the Advanced Vehicles operation was closed, but the Slough factory was taken over by John Wyer and John Willment and run as JW Automotive Engineering, which continued to make and support GT40s. JW also developed the GT40-based, Len Bailey-designed Mirage M1 with its characteristic narrow cockpit to reduce frontal area and drag. The following year, the very different MkIV Fords would win at Le Mans, but then rule changes outlawed the huge V8s.

The new regulations for 1968 introduced a 3.0-litre capacity limit for Group 6 'Prototype' cars, and there was an alternative Group 4 'GT' class with a 5.0-litre limit but subject to a minimum production run of 50 cars (reduced to 25 in 1969). Most people thought the Prototypes would be quicker on most circuits, with the larger-engined GTs having a possible advantage on faster circuits. Alan Mann Racing, which had run

Len Bailey's Ford F3L was beautiful, but ultimately a failure. The DFV-engined sports car was plagued with aerodynamic instability and reliability woes largely attributed to engine vibration.

its own team of GT40s, convinced Walter Hayes of the need for a new 3.0-litre sports prototype in which the DFV engine would play a central role – not that Keith Duckworth was impressed by the idea, saying that if he'd known they wanted a sports car engine he would have designed one. The new car was variously called the P67 or P68, though most knew it as the 'F3L', for 'Ford 3.0-litre'. Its strikingly beautiful shape was the work of Len Bailey, who had been involved with the GT40 from the beginning and had penned that low-drag Mirage body for JW Automotive.

The F3L was much curvier than the GT40 or the Mirage, more in the mould of the Lola T70 or Ferrari P4 and arguably a more arresting shape than any of them, with its penetrating snout and flowing curves over the front wheels. The low, curved cockpit had gull-wing doors, and merged seamlessly into a long, tapering tail. The shape was said to have a drag coefficient as low as 0.27, but like many low-drag designs it generated rear-end lift which made it unstable at high speeds. The F3L had an aluminium monocoque cockpit section behind which the DFV was mounted in a tubular subframe. Suspension was by F1-style wishbones and the rear wheels were driven through a Hewland DG300 five-

RIGHT: *At the Nürburgring 1000km the Ford team has no idea of the troubles that await it. Walter Hayes finds it all very amusing, but something is worrying driver Frank Gardner…*

BELOW: *The Alan Mann F3L waits in the Nürburgring paddock with its engine cover removed, showing off its DFV engine.*

RIGHT: *Chris Irwin shook up the established drivers in Formula 1 in 1967, but at the Nürburgring the following year aerodynamic instability led his F3L to flip over. Although Irwin recovered from his injuries, it ended his racing career.*

speed gearbox – the letters in the designation standing for nothing more romantic than 'Different Gearbox'!

Jim Clark was supposed to give the F3L its debut at the six-hour BOAC 500 sports car race at Brands Hatch on 7 April 1968. Then Colin Chapman decided his star driver's talents were better employed giving his new sponsors, John Player, some extra exposure in a Formula 2 race at Hockenheim that same day. Two F3Ls, resplendent in the usual red and gold Alan Mann livery, were at Brands for Bruce McLaren/Denny Hulme and Mike Spence/Jochen Rindt. Chassis 01 suffered an engine failure in practice and did not start, while 02 was so new it had not turned a wheel before the meeting, but went well in practice. McLaren recorded second fastest time behind the Porsche 907 of Jo Siffert/Hans Herrmann. As the cars lined up on the grid to start the race, news began to filter through from Germany that Jim Clark had crashed his F2 Lotus and been killed. Walter Hayes was in the pits at Brands Hatch when he heard. Mike Spence wondered what chance the rest of the drivers had if an accident could claim a genius like Clark. Ironically just a month later he, too, would die from injuries sustained during a racing accident.

At Brands that day, Spence shared the driving of the one remaining F3L with Bruce McLaren, the New Zealander taking the first stint and disputing the lead with a pair of works Porsches. Spence then took over, but just short of two hours into the race an inner driveshaft coupling failed and the free end of driveshaft ripped into the DFV's exhaust system and the engine subframe. The F3L coasted to a halt on the outside of Clearways, its race run, and to avoid a long walk back to the pits Spence picked his moment and ran across the track to the infield. The BOAC 500 was won by Jacky Ickx and Brian Redman in the JW GT40 chassis 1075, the car that would win Le Mans later in the year and repeat the feat in 1969.

The next race for the F3L was the Nürburgring 1000km, which saw rising star Chris Irwin and the mercurial Pedro Rodriguez paired in one car with Frank Gardner and Richard Attwood in the other. Irwin had made his name at the French Grand Prix the previous year, where he had lapped quicker in a 2.5-litre Tasman BRM than Stewart had in the H16 – so the two drivers had swapped cars, and Irwin had gone even faster in the H16! But his association with the F3L was an unhappy one: in practice, Irwin's car flipped at Flugplatz and plunged into a ditch, the unlucky driver suffering severe head injuries from which he would recover, but which would end his promising racing career. The remaining car retired early due to failing brakes, sealing a miserable weekend for the Alan Mann team. At Spa, a week later, the F3L proved its speed in Frank Gardner's hands, taking pole position by four seconds from the Ickx/ Redman GT40, but retired on the first lap with an engine failure. It was a similar story at the Tourist Trophy meeting at Oulton Park a week later. Richard Attwood put F3L chassis 02 on pole ahead of Jo Bonnier's Chevrolet-engined Lola T70, only to retire in the race with transmission trouble. At Silverstone at the end of June, Gardner lined up second on the grid behind the eventual winner, Denny Hulme's Lola T70, but the F3L was again eliminated by engine problems.

An open-topped version called the P69 was constructed during the winter of 1968/69. It appeared at the BOAC 500 in April, but was withdrawn after engine trouble. Frank Gardner and Denny Hulme drove F3L chassis 03, qualifying seventh but retiring after 14 laps with failing oil pressure. A month later at Silverstone, Gardner put the F3L on pole with a lap nearly two seconds faster than Redman in the best of the Lola-Chevrolets, but before the race could start rain got into the electrics and caused a misfire, so the F3L was withdrawn. It was the last in a string of mishaps which prevented the F3L from fulfilling its potential. Walter Hayes had grown to hate it, and Ford decided instead to concentrate on F1 and rallying.

But the F3L was just the start of the DFV's career in endurance racing, whatever Keith Duckworth's misgivings may have been about the suitability of the engine. While the F3L was still a recent memory Alain de Cadenet's Ecurie Evergreen team installed a DFV in a McLaren M8C Can-Am chassis and ran it in sports car events from 1970, often with Chris Craft and Trevor Taylor sharing the driving duties. Much later de Cadenet would turn in stirring performances in DFV-powered sports cars, first Lolas and later his own cars badged as de Cadenets, in which he would finish third at Le

TOP: *Fast forward to 2003 and David Piper's F3L appears at the Goodwood Festival of Speed, again with its engine cover removed.*

MIDDLE: *F3L's engine bay in 2003 lacks the regulation spare wheel of 1968. Note also the full air filters over the DFV's intake trumpets.*

BOTTOM: *Len Bailey designed one of the most dramatic and purposeful racing car shapes for the F3L. This is the car owned and campaigned until recently by David Piper.*

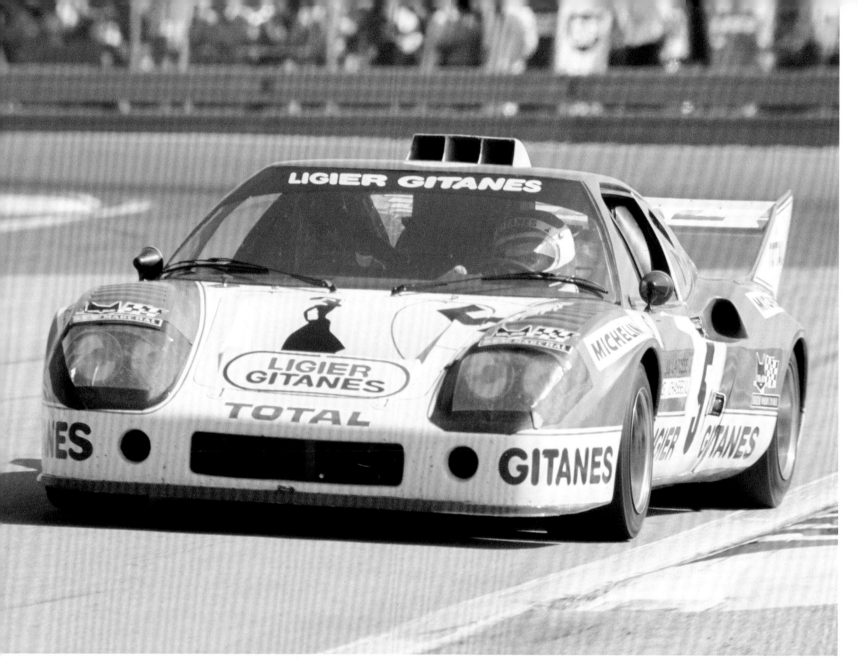

Guy Ligier's JS2 started life as a road car with a Maserati V6 engine, but was later developed as a sports racing car with a DFV engine. This example, driven by Jean-Louis Lafosse and Guy Chasseuil finished second at Le Mans in 1975.

Mans in 1976 and win two World Championship sports car races in 1980.

Guy Ligier was another to employ DFV power in sports car racing. Ligier had been a French rowing champion and a rugby player on the verge of full international status, switched to motorcycle racing and then car racing, and once he had made a fortune in the construction business he became racing car constructor. Ligier's first car was the JS1 designed by Michel Tetu in 1969, the initials in memory of his friend Jo Schlesser who died in a crash at Rouen in 1968 in the air-cooled Honda. The JS1 was a mid-engined sports coupé with a

Lotus-like steel backbone chassis and double-wishbone suspension all round, clothed in a Frua-designed glassfibre body. Initially, power came from a four-cylinder Cosworth FVA engine, and later Ligier tried tuned Ford Cologne V6s. The JS1 won some minor events in 1969 and 1970, but retired early from the Le Mans 24-hours with a distributor failure.

In 1970, Ligier introduced the JS2 road car, using the Maserati V6 from the Citroën SM. For 1971 Tetu penned an open-top sports-racing car, the JS3, with an innovative aluminium honeycomb chassis which incorporated a DFV engine as a stressed member. After an eye-catching

performance at the Le Mans test days in April and a win in a sports car event at Montlhéry, the JS3 went to Le Mans to be driven by Ligier and a young Patrick Depailler. Although it was still running at the end of the race, the JS3 had been delayed by a long gearbox rebuild and was so far behind the leaders that it was not classed as a finisher. Ligier then concentrated on the Maserati-powered JS2, but for Le Mans in 1975 he returned to Cosworth, fitting DFV engines into a pair of JS2s. Alongside them was a lone Maserati-engined entry for Jean-Pierre Jarier and Jean-Pierre Beltoise, which qualified six seconds behind the slower of the Cosworth-engined cars. Jean-Louis Lafosse and Guy Chasseuil brought their JS2-Cosworth home in second place, a lap down on the victorious Gulf GR8 of Derek Bell and Jacky Ickx. But Ligier was soon heading in a different direction, taking his team into F1 with the Matra-engined JS5.

The Gulf Racing GR8 that won at Le Mans in 1975 was the culmination of a project which John Wyer had started in 1969. After toying with the idea of making a bid for the promising but unsorted Alan Mann Ford F3L, JW Automotive instead began work on a 3.0-litre 'Prototype' of its own. John Wyer was unable to secure the services of Len Bailey, who was now working with

OPPOSITE: *Changes in*
sports car regulations
pushed the emphasis on
to 3.0-litre cars for 1972.
After two seasons racing
Porsche 917s, John Wyer's
Gulf-supported team
returned to Ford-powered
cars with a new Cosworth-
engined Mirage M6.

BELOW: *With Cosworth*
power the Ligier JS2
finished second at Le
Mans in 1975, behind a
DFV-engined Mirage.

Alan Mann on the F3L and P69, and Eric Broadley wanted the new car to be a Lola, so Wyer engaged Len Terry to design the Mirage M2.

Cosworth DFV power was considered from the start, but with more and more Formula 1 teams jumping on the DFV bandwagon – not to mention the need to supply Ford's officially-sanctioned F3L project – engines were in short supply. Instead, Walter Hayes revealed to John Wyer that a new 3.0-litre V12 was being developed for Ford by Harry Weslake, and in the meantime JW Automotive looked at alternative 3.0-litre units, including Brabham's Repco V8, and BRM's V12. Terry had just designed new V12 Formula 1 cars for BRM, so it is perhaps no surprise that the BRM V12 was chosen to power the new Mirage. It was running by August 1968, but an 'off' in testing and problems with the handling delayed its public appearance until Daytona the following February. Even then, JW Automotive preferred to race its GT40s, as it did at Sebring – where 'old faithful' GT40 1075 won the race in the hands of Jacky Ickx and Jack Oliver.

The Mirage raced for the first time at Brands Hatch in April, where a driveshaft failure sidelined it after 88 laps (not too dissimilar to the F3L's debut in the same race a year earlier). JW Automotive missed the Monza 1000km and Targa Florio, then returned to racing with the M2s at Spa – where Jacky Ickx put his car on the front row in qualifying, only to retire after 11 laps with fuel system troubles. The sister car of David Hobbs and Mike Hailwood finished seventh, six laps down on the winning Siffert/Redman Porsche.

At the Nürburgring three weeks later, JW Automotive again campaigned a pair of M2s. Hobbs and Hailwood were again paired in their Spa car, still with a BRM V12 engine, while the Ickx/Oliver M2 had been converted to Cosworth DFV power – necessitating chassis and body modifications to get the short, but wide, V8 to fit. Walter Hayes had given up on the F3L project, so now there was no political opposition to JW Automotive using DFVs in their cars, and two engines were loaned to the Slough team. Despite the DFV's power, neither Ickx nor Oliver could get anywhere near the fastest qualifying times (by Siffert's Porsche and Amon's Ferrari) and their race finished prematurely with a front suspension failure. The BRM-engined car lasted another two laps before the fuel pump failed.

At Le Mans, JW Automotive fell back on the reliable GT40s and earned a remarkable second successive victory for 1075. Then, at Watkins Glen, a new open-top Mirage, the M3, was entered for Ickx, its DFV engine breaking a camshaft in the third hour. The team went to Zeltweg in August with stronger suspension and a lower engine position in an effort to improve the handling. Ickx qualified on pole ahead of the Scuderia Filipinetti Lola of Jo Bonnier and Herbert Müller, then set the fastest lap before retiring when a badly welded steering joint failed. JW Automotive consoled themselves with a win at Imola in September in a non-championship race. By then the team was looking forward to the Porsche 917s that it would race, with enormous success, in 1970 and 1971.

It turned out to be a two-season interlude, and in 1972, Wyer's team returned to the Ford fold. More changes in the sports car regulations had outlawed the 5.0-litre Porsches, and the emphasis had once again switched to 3.0-litre 'Prototypes'. A new Mirage was built, the M6, again using the Cosworth DFV engine. It achieved its first win in May 1973 at the Spa 1000km, where Mike Hailwood shared the driving duties for both the team's entries and achieved the rare distinction of finishing both first and second in the same race!

The team continued to campaign the Mirage M6 into 1974, eventually renaming it the Gulf Research GR7.

In 1975, the Le Mans fuel consumption regulations changed, resulting in the Sarthe classic being left out of the World Championship calendar for the first time since 1956. John Wyer had been trying to retire, but thought his cars stood a good chance of winning Le Mans so that was to be the Gulf team's only race entry that year. The DFV-engined GR8 cars, a development of the GR7 with new low-drag bodywork, were the favourites to win and they didn't disappoint. Derek Bell and Jacky Ickx shared the winning car – the first of their many Le Mans successes together – a lap ahead of the Lafosse/Chasseuil Ligier JS2 and six laps clear of the sister Gulf GR8 of Vern Schuppan and Jean-Pierre Jaussaud. The top three cars were all powered by Cosworth-Ford DFV engines; it was, perhaps, Cosworth's finest hour at Le Mans.

The Gulf-Mirage team was then disbanded, but the cars were taken over by Harley Cluxton's Grand Touring Cars team and a GR8 driven by Jean-Louis Lafosse and François Migault was second at Le Mans in 1976, behind the new turbo flat-six Porsche 936. Alain de Cadenet's DFV-powered Lola was third and the second GR8 of Derek Bell/Vern Schuppan was fifth. In eighth place came a new French DFV-engined machine entered and built by a Le Mans local, driver/constructor Jean Rondeau. The cars were entered under the name of Rondeau's sponsor Inaltera, a French wallpaper manufacturer, who provided a million-franc budget – enough to secure the services of some notable driving talent, in the shape of Jean-Pierre Beltoise and Henri Pescarolo. The French pair finished eighth in the leading Inaltera, while Rondeau himself partnered Christine Beckers and Jean-Pierre Jassaud in the second car, which finished 21st.

They were back the following year with three cars, the best of them finishing fourth in the hands of Rondeau and Jean Ragnotti. But then Rondeau's lucrative sponsorship deal was dissolved as Inaltera rearranged its priorities, and the cars were summarily sold off. The determined Rondeau began again with new cars under his own name, and was back at Le Mans in 1978 where the single Rondeau entry finished ninth, while one of the old Inalteras was 13th. Three Rondeaus were entered in 1979, two of them finishing (in fifth and ninth places) while the third was eliminated in an accident.

Rondeau's big year was 1980. Rule changes limited the rate at which fuel could be added to the cars during pit stops, more than doubling the length of each stop. The maximum size of the fuel tank on the car was also reduced. Top-level opposition was slim, the main turbo

competition coming from a Porsche 908/936 hybrid
prepared by Reinhold Joest, and a gaggle of 935s, along
with the French WM cars powered by 2.6-litre Peugeot
V6s. BMW entered a pair of M1s, and Lancia brought
a trio of turbocharged Montecarlos. DFV-powered
challengers were more in evidence than ever, with Alain
de Cadenet's Lola, a Japanese Dome, and the Lola-based
ACR all lining up. Two more, Nick Faure's ex-de Cadenet
Lola and the Hesketh-based Ibec, failed to qualify.

Heavy rain before the race left the circuit wet and
slippery for the early laps. The Porsches of Bob Wollek
and John Fitzpatrick splashed around in the lead chased
by Hans Stuck's BMW, but slowly the Joest Porsche and
the Henri Pescarolo/Jean Ragnotti Rondeau M379B
climbed up the leader board. When the Porsche broke
a fuel injection pump belt the Rondeau took the lead,
while the sister car driven by Rondeau and Jean-Pierre
Jaussaud moved into second place. But the Pescarolo/
Ragnotti car was out early on Sunday morning with
a blown engine, leaving the second Rondeau to fight
it out with the Porsche, driven by Jacky Ickx, Michel
Leclere and Reinhold Joest himself. The Porsche was
delayed by half an hour when it stopped for attention
to the gearbox, after which Ickx set off in pursuit of the

ABOVE: *Jean Rondeau
built cars under the
Inaltera banner, then
used his own name.
He drove his own
Rondeau M379B to
victory at Le Mans in
1980.*

LEFT: *Le Mans 1975,
and the third-placed
Schuppan/Jaussaud
Gulf GR8, with
Jaussaud driving,
makes room for
the second-placed
Ligier JS2 of Lafosse
and Chasseuil. The
top three finishers
were all powered
by Cosworth DFV
engines.*

Rondeau. More rain in the closing stages led to anxious moments for both teams as both leading cars slid off the road, but ultimately it was the Rondeau which emerged the victor, two laps ahead of the Porsche.

It would be Rondeau's only victory at Le Mans, although the team would go on to develop sports-racing cars into the coming era of Group C and ground-effect, all powered by the Cosworth DFV engine. In 1982 they finished second to Porsche in the World Endurance Championship. But it all came to an end when Jean Rondeau was killed in a road accident: a railway crossing was opened for a police car to cross and the impatient Rondeau followed it across, and was hit by the oncoming train. His team was disbanded soon after.

Already another era of DFV-family engines in endurance racing had begun under the Group C rules, which imposed limits on fuel consumption and fuel tank capacity, but no limits on engine size. The exact requirements took a long time to finalise, but once the outline of the Group C rules had been published Cosworth envisaged a larger-capacity version of the DFV, producing more power but still able to run within the fuel-economy constraints likely to be imposed by the rules. Meanwhile, Ford had taken the decision to build

its own car for the new Group C sports car regulations – a project which had started life with British sports car privateer Alain de Cadenet and Len Bailey, the designer who had been involved with the GT40 and then the F3L in the 1960s. It was to be known as the C100, derived from Group C's overall height regulation of 100cm.

The larger, endurance-racing version of the DFV (to be known as the DFL) would be the ideal power unit. Ford paid Cosworth £100,000 to develop the DFL – the same figure, of course, that had been involved in the original DFV project back in 1966, although the effects of inflation meant it represented a significantly smaller investment the second time around. The engine would again have 'Ford' on the cam covers, this time in the form of the famous oval badge.

The DFL project was originally split into three phases. First, Cosworth would develop a 3.3-litre derivative of the DFV which retained the standard stroke but had larger bores. Initially, pistons from the BDG Formula 2 engine were adopted, but later an improved piston was created specifically for the 3.3-litre DFL. The next stage was to build a long-stroke engine which retained the standard bores, producing a 3.6-litre unit. Both strategies for increasing the DFV's capacity had already been employed by outside engine builders, and big-capacity DFVs had been used successfully in hillclimbing where their extra low-rev torque was a considerable advantage when accelerating out of tight, low-speed corners. But this was the first time Cosworth itself had investigated the potential for increasing the displacement of its long-running V8. So it was only when the long-stroke and big-bore engines had been proven that Cosworth combined the wider bore and longer stroke to produce a 3.95-litre V8, the third stage of the project.

Unfortunately, the final Group C regulations allowed far more fuel per race than had been expected, and even the 3.95-litre DFL – which was expected to deliver around 570bhp in full-developed form – would be unlikely to use all the fuel available. At Cosworth thoughts turned to a new avenue of development, turbocharging, but in the meantime the normally aspirated engine was readied for competition.

The C100 had also been hampered by the delay in finalising the Group C rules, and changes to the overall dimensions of the car only added to the early teething troubles. The C100's debut had been scheduled for the Silverstone Six Hours in May 1981, but all sorts of problems – particularly with the bodywork – delayed the Ford's first appearance until the Brands Hatch 1,000km race at the end of September. Formula 2 charger Manfred Winkelhock and 1979 Le Mans winner Klaus Ludwig were engaged to drive the car, Winkelhock putting it on pole a clear half-second faster than the only other Group C car in the race, a reworked Porsche 917 entered by the Kremer brothers. The C100 led the race for the first hour, but was then forced to retire with a gearbox failure.

The 1982 season saw a string of embarrassingly high-profile failures for the C100. At the first round of the World Endurance Championship, the Monza 1,000km, the C100 retired after just 18 laps when a water pipe fractured and the engine over heated. The race was won by Henri Pescarolo and Georgio Francia in a Cosworth-engined Rondeau. At Silverstone Ludwig and Winkelhock survived a litany of problems to finish eighth, 50 miles behind the winning Lancia. At the Nürburgring, the C100 was quick in practice and led the race easily until the differential failed. Then came Le Mans, where it was hoped that the Ford/Porsche battles of the 1960s were to be re-enacted.

Ford had now placed the C100s with Erich Zakowski's Zakspeed concern in an effort to raise the standards of preparation and, with them, the reliability of the cars. The original C100 was joined by a new chassis, and both of them were equipped with 3.95-litre DFLs. Marc Surer and Klaus Ludwig were paired in the new car, while Manfred Winkelhock and a Zakspeed regular, Klaus Niedzwiedz, shared the older car. But neither C100 made it into Sunday: the Winkelhock/Niedzwiedz car lost time with a clutch change, then lost its engine while the Surer/Ludwig car retired with an ignition failure.

Two of the DFL-powered Rondeaus also retired with the same fault. Later it was found that the crankshaft dampers which had been fitted to the DFL engines had failed and the outer mass ring of the damper had severed the wires to the ignition pick-up. The crankshaft dampers, ironically, had been added to the specification to avoid reliability problems. With a longer stroke but conrods the same length as the DFV, the DFL had considerably higher secondary vibrations which caused problems with engine mountings. At critical points in the rev-range some of the drivers also reported that the extra vibration made it difficult for them to breathe. Vibration problems continued throughout the season, but at Brands Hatch later that year the C100s finally showed their potential. Three were entered, and though the Niedzwiedz/Winkelhock car was eliminated early

Expanded in bore and stroke, the DFL endurance engine displaced almost 4.0-litres – but high levels of vibration wreaked havoc with the cars and their drivers.

Manfred Winkelhock and Klaus Niedzwiedz finished 18th in their C100 at Spa in 1982.

LEFT: *Under the watchful eye of Cosworth's Dick Scammell, a turbo DFL is installed in a C100 chassis. The huge turbocharger sits on a parts trolley, waiting to be fitted.*

BELOW: *Monza 1,000km, 1982: another in a string of failures for the C100. The Klaus Ludwig/ Manfred Winklebock/ Marc Surer Ford overheated after just 18 laps. The shocking pink Porsche 935 in the background, driven by Rolf Stommelen and Ted Field, finished second.*

on in an accident, Jonathan Palmer and Desirée Wilson finished a fine fourth with Ludwig/Surer a lap behind in fifth place.

Tony Southgate revised the C100 for 1983, with new bodywork in short-tail and long-tail forms. Although tests at Paul Ricard early in 1983 were conducted with a normally aspirated 3.95-litre DFL, the intention was to fit the turbocharged version of the engine which Cosworth was now developing. Ford Motorsport, under the control of Karl Ludvigsen, announced that the C100s would not race until the turbo engine was ready. Cosworth was working on a relatively simple and lightweight single-turbo installation, with low boost pressure and a target power output of 700bhp at a modest 8,500rpm. In addition, development work was under way on a solution for the vibration problems which had always been a headache with DFV-family engines, and which were particularly troublesome with DFLs. Twin Lanchester-type balance shafts were added to smooth out the vibrations, while much work also went into the design and testing of new, more reliable crankshaft dampers.

Just a few weeks after the announcement that the 1983 C100s would race when the turbo DFL was ready,

RIGHT: *The C100 was a high-profile failure for Ford – late, unreliable and under-achieving. Zakspeed later redeveloped it into the C1, and used it in German national championship events.*

BELOW: *The Cosworth V8 had a successful run in Group C2 racing in the 1980s. This is the Spice SE88C of Gordon Spice, Ray Bellm and Pierre de Thoisy, winning class C2 at Le Mans in 1988.*

Karl Ludvigsen moved on, and Ford Motorsport came under the control (again) of Stuart Turner. Things rapidly changed: the C100's international programme was shelved, along with the development programme for Ford's RS1700T rally car. Instead Zakspeed campaigned the cars in German national events and evolved the design into the C1, powered by a derivative of the four-cylinder turbo engine from its successful racing Capris. That was effectively the end of the DFV family's endurance racing career at the highest level, although a Rondeau or de Cadenet Lola would continue to pop up at odd events. While Porsche's 956 dominated Group C, the Cosworth DFL (in both 3.3-litre or 3.95-litre forms) continued to provide motive power for Spice, Ecurie Ecosse, Tiga and others in a new C2 class run to tighter fuel consumption limits.

One more Cosworth-engined endurance car is worthy of mention, even though it never raced. In 1978, Jean Rondeau revealed plans for the M579, a new Group 6 sports car, which was remarkable for having six wheels – four at the front in the manner of Tyrrell's Project 34 F1 car. It was to be powered by a 630bhp Cosworth DFX turbo engine. The M579, perhaps predictably, never progressed beyond the scale-model stage.

SUPERVAN

Promoting commercial vehicles must be largely a humourless business, but Ford shook up the status quo in 1971 with a vehicle called Supervan built by Terry Drury Racing. Fat slick tyres sat inside the extended wheel arches of the Transit van bodyshell, hinting at what lay beneath: GT40 running gear and a mid-mounted 5.0-litre Ford V8 developing 400bhp. It made its debut at the Easter Monday meeting at Brands Hatch in 1971 and did the rounds of the motoring press, who were suitably amazed at a Transit with a GT40's bellow and a top speed of around 150mph.

The concept was revisited in 1984 with Supervan 2. This time the body was a glassfibre replica of a Mark 2 Transit, with a deep front air dam and huge air ducts in the flanks. The underpinnings came from a Ford C100 – complete with Cosworth DFL engine. Built by Auto Racing Technology of Woolaston, Supervan 2 was unveiled at the first British Truck Grand Prix at Donington Park in 1984. Later, at Silverstone, it was timed at 174mph. But Supervan 2's promotional value was limited, because a new 'fast front' Transit was introduced at the end of 1985. Supervan 2 ended up in the Leyland truck museum in Lancashire.

In 1994, it was given a new lease of life – and a new name, Supervan 3. The body was replaced by a seven-eighths scale replica of the latest Transit, painted in Ford Motorsport's blue and white livery. It was powered by a 650bhp Cosworth HB engine, the 75-degree, 3.5-litre V8 designed for use in Formula 1 by Benetton and later employed in TWR's XJR-14 Group C car. Much later, Supervan 3 was refurbished to take part in celebrations for the Transit's 40th anniversary, including an appearance at the Goodwood Festival of Speed. A 3.0-litre V6 Pro-Sports engine was fitted. As this book goes to press it seems likely that Supervan 3 will soon be rebuilt into a C100 for historic racing – and the most famous Transit of all will be no more.

Supervan 2, based on a C100 chassis complete with Cosworth DFL engine, made its debut in 1984 and hit 174mph in tests at Silverstone. It was later rebodied, re-engined and renamed Supervan 3.

CHAPTER EIGHT

DFX: COSWORTH'S TURBO INDYCAR ENGINE

There are few families of race engines in the history of motorsport that can claim a longer competitive career than Cosworth's DFV, but one that can is the Offenhauser in-line four. Designed by Fred Offenhauser for Harry Miller in 1930 as a boat racing engine, it was adapted for auto racing in 1933. When Miller's company failed later that year, Offenhauser and another Miller engineer, Leo Goossen, bought the rights to the engine and continued development. The 'Offy' became the standard engine for American open-wheel oval racing. After the war Offenhauser sold out to three-time Indy 500 winner Louis Meyer and his partner Dale Drake, who continued to refine and rework the Offy design as the Indy racing regulations changed over the years. The Offy won every Indy 500 in the 1950s, and on several occasions every one of the starters used it.

In 1964, Drake took over the running of the company, while Meyer concentrated on tuning and rebuilding Ford's new stock-block V8 racing engines. Jim Clark began a run of success for the Ford V8 with a win in the Lotus-Ford 38 at Indianapolis in 1965, but soon turbocharged Offenhauser engines were under development – and once the teething troubles were fixed, the turbo Offys proved almost unbeatable. Turbo versions of the four-cam Fords were also produced, but

Rutherford's challenge for a second consecutive Indy 500 win in 1981 ended early with a fuel-pump failure.

compared with the Offenhausers they were big, heavy and had a high centre of gravity, and most teams stuck with the turbo four.

Work on another alternative to the Offy began as far back as 1972, when Roger Penske asked Cosworth to build a batch of short-stroke, low-compression DFVs with a view to turbocharging them – but the project was never completed. Around the same time Parnelli Jones and Vel Miletich founded their 'Vel's Parnelli Jones' team which started by running Indy cars and branched out into Formula 5000 (which used 5.0-litre stock-block engines) and Formula 1. It was this connection between American oval racing and the DFV-dominated arena of F1 which would see the turbocharged Cosworth V8 project come to fruition.

The Parnelli team's first F1 car, the VPJ4, was designed by Maurice Philippe and used a conventional aluminium monocoque structure with a Cosworth DFV engine and Hewland transaxle. It had more than a passing resemblance to the Lotus 72, a previous Maurice Philippe design, but suffered from over-soft suspension and a lack of serious development. The VPJ4 made its race debut at the Canadian Grand Prix in 1974 in Mario Andretti's capable hands, and finished seventh after a

ABOVE: *Ford's Indy V8 of the early 1960s was much bigger and heavier than the later DFV. This is a 1963 engine with pushrod valve operation, but later engines had twin overhead camshafts on each cylinder bank.*

RIGHT: *Ford entered USAC racing in 1963 with a 4.2-litre V8 engine for Team Lotus. Here, Jim Clark in his 'funny car' Lotus 29 leads one of the old-fashioned 'roadsters', with its front-mounted four-cylinder Offenhauser engine, in the Milwaukee 500.*

OPPOSITE: *Jim Clark won the Indianapolis 500 in this Lotus 38 in 1965, forcing the USAC racing teams to take mid-engined chassis and the Ford engine seriously. It would be the beginning of a revolution in USAC racing.*

RIGHT: *With the advent of turbochargers, the Offy engine fought back – but the big Ford V8 was still a force in USAC racing. This is 1971, and Al Unser's Parnelli-Ford is on the way to winning his second consecutive Indy 500.*

BELOW: *A detailed illustration of the Cosworth DFX engine.*

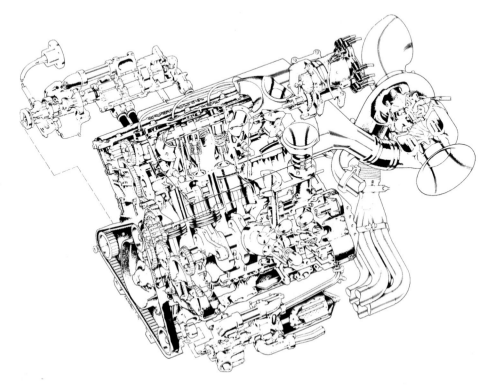

long battle with Denny Hulme's McLaren. It was also the first race for Mark Donohue's Penske PC1, which finished eighth. At Watkins Glen the Parnelli's soft suspension worked well over the bumps and Andretti claimed a second-row grid slot, just two tenths of a second behind Reutemann's Brabham-Ford – but was disqualified from the race after receiving outside assistance. The team was back in F1 in 1975, and during that season Andretti finished third in the International Trophy, recorded fastest lap in the shortened Spanish Grand Prix, then finished fourth in Sweden, but there was little else for them to cheer.

In USAC racing the Parnelli team had also been struggling, giving up on their own chassis and instead running customer Eagle chassis fitted with turbocharged Offenhauser engines. The engines were proving unreliable, and at the same time expensive to build and maintain, in contrast to the reliability and relatively low cost of the Cosworth V8 in Parnelli's F1 machine. Miletich started to investigate turbocharging the DFV to make an IndyCar engine, and engine builder Larry Slutter and machine operator Chickie Hiroshima were set to work. To bring the capacity down below the 2.65-litre limit they used the short-stroke crankshaft which had been developed by Cosworth for the abortive Penske project, and they adapted cam profiles which had been used with the four-cam US Ford V8s. When the new engine was tested in the autumn of 1974 it instantly produced more power than the turbo Offy, though making it reliable was a more difficult problem. Cooling was a major issue, and as a first step the water pump was upgraded to deliver a much higher flow rate of cooling water.

Parnelli had new VPJ6 cars in Viceroy liveries ready for Al Unser and Mario Andretti at the Indy 500 practice sessions in May 1975. However, this 'new' machine was little more than the VPJ4 Formula 1 chassis with the narrower wheels demanded by Indy rules and the turbocharged DFV V8, and it suffered from the same handling problems that troubled the VPJ4. Despite the extra power and the much smoother power delivery of the Cosworth engine, the team preferred its Offy-engined Eagles for the race, although neither driver was on the pace. But Unser reappeared in the VPJ6 at Phoenix in November 1975 and finished an encouraging fifth. For the first round of the 1976 USAC championship Unser was back at Phoenix again, this time in a car which had been revised by Parnelli's new designer, John Barnard, and with new sponsorship from American

Racing Wheels. The USAC faithful were surprised to see Unser qualify on pole in the VPJ6B, and the new car survived to finish fourth. Unser qualified fourth at Indianapolis and brought the VPJ6 home seventh, and at the Pocono 500 in June he recorded the first win for the Parnelli and the turbocharged Cosworth V8. He would win twice more that year, at the Milwaukee 200 and the Phoenix 150.

The Vel's Parnelli Jones team continued to campaign the VPJ6B in 1977, Danny Ongais winning in Michigan and Al Unser winning in Ontario. But now the Parnelli was not the only Cosworth-engined car in the USAC field. McLaren had produced a new car, the M24, which won six USAC events that year. Five of those wins went to Johnny Rutherford in the works Team McLaren entry, but the champion that year was the super-consistent Tom Sneva, who won at the Texas World Speedway in his Penske-entered car, and retained the title the following year despite failing to win a single championship event.

Although early development work on the turbo engine had been carried out by Parnelli's own team and Cosworth had shown only a passing interest, Keith Duckworth was now seeing Niki Lauda and Ferrari become a forceful competitor in Formula 1, and was

starting to worry that the DFV's days as a Grand Prix winner might be nearing their end. The turbocharged USAC engine was showing promise, so it seemed like a good diversification for Cosworth to begin building their own 'official' version. Cosworth established a satellite operation in the USA – in Torrance, California, near Parnelli's workshops – which was to be run by Larry Slutter who had been tempted away from the Parnelli team. At first, Slutter's task was to arrange for the supply of components to Northampton so that Cosworth could build complete turbo engines, where previously it had merely built short-stroke, low-compression DFVs and supplied them to the USA for conversion to turbo units. The new engine was known as the DFX.

Development work concentrated on raising the power output, improving reliability and also attempting to improve drivability. On superspeedway ovals the sudden delivery of the turbo engine was less of an issue, but on road courses like Long Beach it was more of a problem, particularly if the track was wet. Cosworth produced new pistons with thicker crowns, necessitating changes to the gudgeon pins and connecting rods, and new heads with the exhaust valves further apart to allow larger cooling water jackets around the exhaust valve seat area.

The American Hilborn fuel injection system was heavily modified, and eventually replaced entirely with a new system designed by Cosworth. The new injection system was known as the 'monovalve', because it had a single throttle butterfly behind the turbo compressor, replacing the slide throttles used on the DFV.

Already the DFX had broken the domination of the turbo Offy, which won only three times in 1977 and twice in 1978. More and more teams adopted turbo Cosworth power, but a few remained loyal to other engines for a little longer. A. J. Foyt's turbocharged Coyote, powered by a reworked version of the 1960s four-cam Ford V8, won three races in 1977, one in 1978 and one more in 1979, but eventually Foyt switched to a 'customer' Parnelli VPJ6B with a Cosworth DFX. Al Unser recorded the DFX's first Indianapolis 500 victory driving a Lola in 1978 and finished the year with a 'triple crown' of 500-mile victories. The DFX scored its first American championship win in 1979, when veteran Foyt won four USAC races with the Parnelli to wrap up his seventh USAC title – in a season dominated by unrest at the top of the American motor racing establishment.

Many of the teams had become disillusioned with the way the United States Auto Club ran IndyCar racing, with its complex and curious rules, and pronouncements that often seemed arbitrary and inconsistent. For 1979, boost pressures were severely restricted, from 80in of mercury (about 39psi boost) to 50in of mercury (about 25psi boost). The idea was intended to give cheaper stock-block engines (and the old turbo Offy, which was allowed more boost) a chance of competing against the turbo Cosworths – but actually the lower boost pressure helped to improve the DFX's reliability and made it even more dominant. That season many of the team owners banded together to form CART (Championship Auto Racing Teams) which was the IndyCar equivalent of the Formula 1 Constructors Association, FOCA. When the USAC turned down CART's suggestions for improvements to its racing series, CART broke away from the USAC and organised its own championship. To complicate matters, the USAC retained control of the most famous American race of all, the Indianapolis 500.

Rick Mears won the first CART championship in 1979, driving for Roger Penske in a car powered, inevitably, by a Cosworth DFX engine. Mears also won at Indy in that year. In 1980 both the classic Indy 500 race and the CART title fell to Johnny Rutherford, driving for fellow Texan Jim Hall's Chaparral team. That season Hall

ABOVE: *Rolling towards the green flag at Indianapolis, 1980: Johnny Rutherford's Chaparral 2K is alongside the Penskes of Mario Andretti and Bobby Unser.*

LEFT: *Texan Johnny Rutherford stops for fuel and tyres on the way to victory at Indianapolis in 1980. 'Lone Star JR' is driving John Barnard's famous ground-effect Chaparral 2K.*

RIGHT: *Roger Penske's pit crew goes to work on Bobby Unser's car at Atlanta in 1981. Although the season would be successful for Penske, it would be Unser's team-mate Rick Mears who ended the year as CART champion.*

BELOW: *Mears won back-to-back CART titles in 1981 and 1982 driving for Roger Penske, with six wins in the first year and four the second – all powered by the now-ubiquitous Cosworth DFX engine.*

introduced the Chaparral 2K, designed by John Barnard and incorporating the ground-effect aerodynamic principles which had been proven in Formula 1 in 1978 by the Lotus 79. Rutherford had won from pole position in the Chaparral's first race, at Ontario, and won four more races that season to take a dominant series victory. The Mears/Penske/Cosworth combination returned to the fore in the CART championship in 1981 and 1982, winning 10 of the 22 races over those two seasons. The Indy 500 – still not part of the championship due to the CART/USAC wrangles – was another success for Penske in 1981, this time with Bobby Unser at the wheel. Gordon Johncock won at Indy for the Patrick Racing team in 1982, powered of course by a DFX engine.

The Penske-Cosworths won the championship again in 1983. This time the winning driver was Al Unser, who won just one race – at Cleveland in July – but scored points consistently to win the title, despite Teo Fabi's four race victories in the Forsythe March-Cosworth. Another March-Cosworth, run by the Bignotti-Cotter team and driven by Tom Sneva, won the Indy 500. Mario Andretti took the championship in a Carl Haas Lola-Cosworth in 1984, while Rick Mears won the big race in a

Penske March. A March-Cosworth was again the machine to have in 1985, and Danny Sullivan proved it with a famous win in the Indy 500 after spinning out of the lead and then fighting back to beat Mario Andretti. Al Unser's March won the championship that year. Bobby Rahal's championship victory and Indy 500 win in 1986 were more successes for March but Rahal and the Truesports team switched to Lola chasis for 1987, and won another championship. That year Al Unser crashed his Penske March in practice for the Indy 500 and the team rescued a year-old March chassis that was on display in a hotel lobby in Pasadena, prepped it for the race – and Unser won! By the end of 1987 the DFX had won nine straight CART championships and ten Indianapolis 500 races.

By the mid-1980s, going CART racing without a Cosworth engine, and preferably a March chassis, was almost unheard of. Cosworth was in the happy position of a near-monopoly in the sport, and had agreed with team owners that development of the DFX would be deliberately limited to keep costs down. But that inevitably left the door open for a new engine which could take advantage of Cosworth's relaxed attitude – and the challengers came from within Cosworth itself.

Two Cosworth engineers, Paul Morgan and Mario Ilien, teamed up to start building their own race engines at Brixworth in Northamptonshire, just down the road from Cosworth in Northampton. Just as the name 'Cosworth' had been formed from its founders' surnames, Ilien and Morgan put their own names together and called their company Ilmor. Morgan had led the DFX development project at Cosworth, while Ilien had been responsible for the update of the DFV to create the short-stroke, narrow valve-angle DFY in 1983. Now they brought much of the experience they had gained with those two projects together in a new IndyCar engine for Roger Penske, who secured funding for the project from General Motors through its Chevrolet brand.

The Ilmor-Chevrolet 265A made its race debut in 1986. Like the DFX it was a 2.65-litre, 90-degree V8 with four valves per cylinder – using cylinder heads which mounted the valves at a very narrow included angle, like the DFY. It clearly used a great deal of the knowledge Morgan and Ilien had gained working on the DFX and DFY projects for Cosworth. Early Ilmor-Chevrolet engines were powerful, but commonly suffered from

Rick Mears began the 1982 CART season with two straight wins. Here, the Penske heads for victory at Phoenix.

timing gear problems – just like the DFV had in its early days – and it was 1987 before the engine became a reliable race-winner. That year, Mario Andretti's Newman-Haas Lola-Chevrolet was on pole for nine of the 15 CART races, and won two of them. Emerson Fittipaldi's Patrick Racing March-Chevrolet added another two wins for Ilmor. Although the CART championship winner – Bobby Rahal in the Truesports Lola – was Cosworth-powered, there was a new and significant challenger in town…

The following year the Ilmor-Chevrolet engine dominated the CART championship, winning all but one of the 15 races – and the only non-Chevrolet victory, at Pocono, went to reigning champion Rahal in a Judd-engined Truesports Lola. Cosworth responded to the Ilmor challenge with the DFS, which drew on the lessons learned with the heavily revised DFR Formula 1 engine which had been produced for Benetton in 1988, and would be used by 'customer' F1 teams until 1991. The DFR had been competitive, if perhaps not the most powerful or the most reliable engine in Formula 1. The DFS has a similar career, notching up a single win in Bobby Rahal's Kraco Lola at Meadowlands in 1989, but never coming close to overhauling the might of the Ilmor-Chevrolets. Cosworth could perhaps draw some

ABOVE: *Al Unser's 1983 Penske-Cosworth won only one race to Teo Fabi's four – but consistent points scoring gave Unser the CART title that year.*

RIGHT: *Danny Sullivan on the way to his 'spin and win' Indy 500 victory in 1985. Sullivan spun out of the lead after 120 laps but managed to keep the Penske-Cosworth out of the wall, then set off in pursuit of new leader Mario Andretti. After 20 laps he was back in front again and heading for a famous win.*

LEFT: *Ilmor's Chevrolet-funded IndyCar engine appeared in 1986, and was winning races in 1987. It ended the DFX's dominance of the sport. This is Mario Andretti on the way to winning the Long Beach Grand Prix in 1987, in the Newman-Haas Lola-Chevrolet.*

BELOW: *Al Unser Jnr won twice in the Shierson March in 1985, and once in 1986, but there were no wins in 1987. Unser switched to Ilmor-Chevrolet power for 1988 with the Galles team, and was soon back in winning form.*

consolation from the fact that other notable motorsport names, including Alfa Romeo, Judd and even Pórsche, found it equally difficult.

The DFX and DFS engines, although born out of the Ford-sponsored DFV project, had never enjoyed financial support from the blue oval. But at the end of 1991, Ford and Cosworth joined forces to produce a new engine for CART/IndyCar racing. The Cosworth XB V8 was built from the start to be a 2.65-litre engine, so it was considerably smaller and lighter than the DFX or DFS – and it had enough potential to woo the reigning champions, the Newman-Haas team, away from Ilmor. Even though 1992 was always going to be a 'development' year, the XB performed extremely well: Michael Andretti won five events and led all but two of the races at some point, finishing second overall in the championship behind Bobby Rahal's Lola-Chevrolet. Despite that promising start, he chose to move to Formula 1 with McLaren in 1993 and was replaced by reigning F1 champion Nigel Mansell, who took Newman-Haas and the XB-engined Lola to the CART/IndyCar title. The days of the DFV family of engines in American racing might have been over, but for Cosworth a new era had already begun.

CHAPTER NINE

BACK TO THE FRONT: THE 3.5-LITRE ENGINES

After 19 seasons and 155 World Championship race victories, the Formula 1 career of the DFV (and its cousin the DFY) had finally come to an end at the close of the 1985 season. Turbocharged engines had taken time to become established in Formula 1, but by the early 1980s it had been easy to see that they offered by far the most potential for development. As the hard-pressed engine development engineers gradually figured out how to make their motors survive greater and greater boost pressures, the power outputs of the turbo engines soared out of the reach of normally aspirated engines like the Cosworth V8s. The 3.0-litre non-turbo engines which had been the mainstay of Formula 1 since 1966 were finally banned at the end of 1985, and F1 adopted turbo engines across the board. Ironically, after years battling to get turbo engines taken seriously in Formula 1, Renault chose this moment to announce its intention to withdraw from the sport as a chassis manufacturer, although its engines continued to power Lotus, Ligier and Tyrrell cars into 1986. By then the best turbo engines were racing with close to 1,000bhp – while qualifying outputs were well in excess of 1,250bhp, all from just 1.5-litres.

Cosworth was now working on more projects than ever, both in racing and in the road-car arena. A twin-cam, 16-valve cylinder head design for Mercedes-Benz had blossomed into a contract for manufacture of the

Tyrrell was the team to beat in the 'atmo' championship in 1987. Jonathan Palmer and Philippe Streiff comfortably won the Colin Chapman Cup for constructors, and Palmer took the Jim Clark Trophy for drivers.

heads. A similar conversion for Ford's ubiquitous 'Pinto' four-cylinder engine, intended to become a conversion kit with a market of a few hundred units a year for competition use, had turned into the YBB turbo engine for the Sierra RS Cosworth with a production run of 5,000 for Group A homologation. Cosworth's reputation, though, was based on its continuing success in Formula 1 and being eased out of top-level motorsport as turbo engines took over must have been an unpleasant prospect. For a time, Keith Duckworth's views on the regulation of turbo engines, and the inadequacy of the equivalence formulas which supposedly provided a level playing field for turbo and normally aspirated engines, prevented him from sanctioning work on a Cosworth turbo engine for F1. But eventually he was persuaded, and predictably it was Walter Hayes – with a little help from Ken Tyrrell – who made the difference.

Early design work on the Cosworth turbo was hampered by proposals for rule changes which seemed to vary by the week. In the end, Cosworth settled on a twin-turbocharged 120-degree V6 which Ford called the TEC (Turbocharged Engine – Cosworth). Cosworth called it the GB, next in line after the GA which had been Cosworth's last V6 engine for Ford – 12 years earlier! The engine went into a new Lola chassis developed for Carl Haas's brand-new F1 team, with Alan Jones and Patrick Tambay as the drivers, but development of the new car and new engine was a long and bumpy road. It didn't help that Haas lost his title sponsor, the American group Beatrice Companies, part of the way through the project after controversial Beatrice CEO Jim Dutt left the company. Beatrice had financed Haas's F1 and IndyCar operations to the tune of $70 million, and without their support both teams struggled for money. The F1 cars were slow and unreliable, but as Cosworth gradually gained in experience with F1 turbo engines, embracing the latest 'rocket fuel' brews which allowed high boost to be used with less chance of detonation, power outputs rose and engine reliability improved. Eventually, though, Ford lost patience with the Haas team and bought themselves out of their contract. Instead, the Ford-Cosworth turbo engine was supplied to Benetton for 1987.

The FIA then did what the FIA has always done best, and changed its mind. After just one season of turbo-only F1 racing in 1986, and after assuring engine builders that the regulations would remain stable for at least five years, the FIA decided that turbo cars were too fast, too dangerous and too expensive. To reduce turbo power outputs a compulsory 'pop-off' valve would be introduced in 1987, limiting boost-pressure to 4.0bar (58psi). That year normally aspirated engines were readmitted to Grands Prix, this time with a 3.5-litre capacity limit and running in cars with a lower minimum weight limit than the turbos. The non-turbo runners would compete in the Drivers' and Constructors' Championships as normal, but they were expected to be at a disadvantage against the turbo cars – except, it was thought, at street circuits like Monaco and Detroit where their lighter weight would count and their lack of top-end power would be no handicap. There would also be separate 'normally-aspirated' championships, the Colin Chapman Trophy for constructors and the Jim Clark Cup for drivers.

With barely six months between the announcement of the new formula and the first race in Brazil in April, there simply wasn't time to design and build a brand-new engine for the 3.5-litre formula. But Cosworth's experience with the DFL endurance-racing engine had shown that it was certainly possible to build a DFV-family engine with larger capacity, so a 3.5-litre version was created to take the venerable V8 back into F1 after

little more than a season on the sidelines. Cosworth combined the larger 90mm bore of the 3.95-litre DFL with a new 68.6mm stroke, tweaked the cylinder heads and valve sizes, and very quickly came up with a 3.5-litre Formula 1 motor which it called the DFZ.

Three teams began the 1987 season with DFZ power. Ken Tyrrell happily turned his back on the complication of Renault turbo engines and embraced a new era of normally aspirated Cosworth power for the Tyrrell DG016 cars, designed on the latest computer-aided design (CAD) equipment thanks to sponsor Data General. Tyrrell retained one of its drivers from 1986, Frenchman Philippe Streiff, but Martin Brundle departed for Zakspeed and was replaced by another Brit, Jonathan Palmer. March returned to F1 as a works team with a single DFZ-powered car for reigning European F3000 champion Ivan Capelli, at first running a modified Formula 3000 car. The other normally aspirated runner was the shoestring AGS outfit, which fielded a single car for F1 debutant Pascal Fabre. All four non-turbo machines were Cosworth-powered.

In Brazil, the Palmer Tyrrell was a full ten seconds off the pace of the turbocharged F1 cars, but it was still comfortably the quickest of the non-turbo competitors.

In the race, Palmer finished tenth, with Streiff's sister car 11th. Fabre was the last running car, six laps down on the winner (Alain Prost's McLaren-TAG), while Capelli's March had suffered from so many engine troubles in practice that the team had run out of working motors, and the car had to be withdrawn from the race. After the first round of the championship Palmer was leading the Jim Clark Cup and Tyrrell was comfortably heading the Colin Chapman Trophy, from AGS.

At the San Marino Grand Prix the non-turbo ranks were swelled by the appearance of a new Ralph Bellamy-designed Lola, run by former Renault boss Gerard Larrousse and occupied by ex-RAM, ex-Ligier driver Philippe Alliot. The Frenchman qualified 21st overall but second in the non-turbo class, behind Streiff in the faster of the two Tyrrells. Capelli ran a 3.3-litre DFL-engined F3000 car in practice, and also debuted the definitive DFZ-engined March 871 F1 car which qualified 22nd. Palmer's Tyrrell DG016 was behind him, after suffering from a misfire throughout the practice sessions. Fabre was last on the grid in the AGS, as he had been in Brazil, and he continued the symmetry by again finishing the race, again driving the last running car, and again ending the race six laps down on the leaders. Philippe Streiff looked set for a creditable ninth place but ended up with an even more creditable eighth after Derek Warwick's Arrows ran out of fuel with two laps to go. Alliot's new Lola was 10th and second in class. Neither Capelli's March nor Palmer's Tyrrell finished the race, the March suffering a rotor-arm failure and the Tyrrell being sidelined by clutch problems.

As a result, Philippe Streiff went to the Belgian Grand Prix at Spa two weeks later as leader of the non-turbo drivers' championship, while Tyrrell held a useful lead over AGS and Lola in the Constructors' Championship. Still plagued by misfires, the two Tyrrells qualified 23rd and 24th at Spa, behind Capelli's March and Alliot's Lola. Fabre was the last of the non-turbo cars on the grid, but remarkably, Alex Caffi's Osella contrived to be even slower, despite the theoretical benefit of Alfa V8 turbo power. At the start, Nigel Mansell's Williams led away, but René Arnoux's Ligier collected Andrea de Cesaris's Brabham at the tight La Source hairpin. Minutes later the race was red-flagged when Philippe Streiff's Tyrrell got away from him through the dauntingly fast Eau Rouge complex and slammed into the Armco. Even worse, Jonathan Palmer in the other Tyrrell was left with nowhere to go and crashed into his team-mate, wrecking both Tyrrells, though happily, without injury to either driver.

Streiff bravely climbed into the one spare Tyrrell, leaving Palmer to sit out the restart, which saw Ayrton Senna's Lotus muscle between the Williams cars of Mansell and Nelson Piquet. But Senna, Mansell and Piquet all retired from the race, leaving the win for Prost's McLaren, which was fortunate to avoid non-turbo winner, Philippe Alliot, as his Lola rejoined the circuit following a closing-laps spin. Streiff's Tyrrell was the second non-turbo car home, ninth overall, and Fabre's AGS was classified tenth despite being halted by electrical problems right at the end of the race. Ivan Capelli's March had retired with wilting oil pressure. Despite losing two cars in that Eau Rouge collision, Tyrrell still had a comfortable lead in both 'atmospheric' championships.

At Monaco, Ken Tyrrell's budget took another pounding when Streiff crashed in practice and then again in the race, cracking a rib in the process. After the disappointment of Spa, Palmer had a much happier race – qualifying 15th, ahead of several turbo cars, and finishing a fine fifth to win the non-turbo class. Capelli was sixth in his March after chasing Palmer hard and, as usual, Fabre was last to finish in the AGS. Alliot's Lola retired with an engine failure. The next race, at the Detroit street circuit, was expected to treat the 3.5-litre cars equally well, but that didn't quite work out: Capelli stopped with electrical trouble, Alliot hit the wall while trying to find a way past Arnoux, and Streiff lost a wheel. So Palmer won the class, despite a pit stop after contact with Patrese's Brabham, while Fabre was 12th and last. Palmer retook the lead in the Jim Clark Trophy with, remarkably, Fabre in second place thanks to his consistent finishes.

For the French Grand Prix at Paul Ricard, the 3.5-litre cars were hampered by their lack of straight-line speed. Despite that, Streiff finished an excellent sixth with his Tyrrell team-mate Palmer seventh, and Fabre once again was last but he at least finished, unlike 17 of the 26 starters – including Alliot, who retired with ignition failure, and Capelli with a blown DFZ engine. For the Italian it was the end of a grim weekend: he had been forced to use the spare March after his race car had, of all things, fallen off its jack in the pit garage and sustained damage to its monocoque which was serious enough to render it unusable.

Palmer extended his championship lead at Silverstone with another class win. Fabre's AGS was the only other non-turbo finisher: Streiff blew an engine, while Capelli's March and Alliot's Lola both suffered from terminal

The DFR was still recognisably a DFV-series engine, but wholesale revisions by Geoff Goddard had resulted in an engine which was 80 per cent brand new. For 1988, the DFR was exclusively supplied to the Benetton team.

transmission troubles. At Hockenheim, another 'power' circuit expected to favour the turbo cars, the two Tyrrells finished just a lap down on Nelson Piquet's winning Williams. After a race-long battle Streiff edged out his team-mate to finish a superb fourth, with Palmer fifth and Alliot's Lola sixth. Fabre's consistent run came to an end after over-revving the DFZ and dropping a valve, while Capelli's engine suffered another broken rotor arm.

Tyrrell wrapped up the Colin Chapman Trophy for constructors, and Palmer extended his Jim Clark Cup lead, with seventh place overall and the class win in Hungary. Streiff finished ninth, and Capelli was tenth in the Leyton House March. Fabre's AGS was back to its slow, but reliable, form in 13th place. Alliot was the only non-turbo non-finisher: the Frenchman spun his Lola on lap two, flat-spotting a tyre, and the resulting vibrations eventually broke a suspension wishbone. He went better in Austria a week later however, where the race was halted twice after start-line pile-ups. The second of those claimed Alliot's race car and he restarted in the T-car, finishing 12th overall and second in class to Ivan Capelli in the spare March. Both Tyrrells had been involved in the start-line shunts, Palmer taking the spare

car this time but finishing only 14th with his DFZ engine misfiring after breaking a valve spring.

Capelli split the Tyrrells at Monza, where Streiff won the non-turbo battle despite a tangle with Alliot which ended the Lola's race. Neither Pascal Fabre in the AGS nor Nicola Larini in the new DFZ-engined Coloni managed to qualify. Coloni missed the Portuguese Grand Prix where Fabre again failed to qualify. Capelli's Leyton House March performed well again, winning the class from a determined Jonathan Palmer. Streiff was third in the class after an early spin, and Alliot retired with a fuel pump failure.

At Jerez, where the track suited the 'atmo' cars, Alliot battled with Palmer for the class win until the Englishman was unceremoniously punted off by Arnoux's Ligier. Alliot went on to win the class with Streiff second and Capelli third. Fabre and Larini both qualified – at the expense of the two Osella-Alfa turbos – but retired early in the race. Alliot won the class again in Mexico where the 7,000ft altitude robbed the atmo cars of power. Palmer was the quicker of the two Tyrrells, second and third in class, and Yannick Dalmas was fourth in the class in a second Larrousse-Lola. But it was a less successful weekend for Capelli, who retired with an engine failure, and Fabre who failed to qualify the AGS. The last two races – Japan and Australia – saw Jonathan Palmer record two more class wins, giving him a convincing victory over his team-mate Philippe Streiff in the Jim Clark Trophy.

By the end of the season the F1 teams knew they were facing more rule changes, together with the usual 'silly season' driver swaps and some changes to the engine and chassis pairings. McLaren was gaining Senna and Honda turbo engines, while Williams was going for Judd 'atmospheric' engines, as were March and Ligier. Minardi was switching from the unreliable power units produced by Motori Moderni to the more dependable Cosworth V8s. Tyrrell, AGS, Larrousse and Coloni were sticking with DFZs and three new teams – Rial, EuroBrun and Scuderia Italia – were adopting Cosworth power.

Benetton also had a new engine for 1988. The latest round of rule changes had reduced the maximum boost pressure of the turbo engines, controlled by the 'pop-off' valve, to 2.5bar (36psi), which it was thought would cut the power output of the turbos from about 850bhp in race trim to nearer 650bhp. The FIA had also given notice that the turbo engines would be outlawed entirely at the end of the season, and all the teams would be required to run 3.5-litre normally aspirated engines in

FORMULA 3000

By 1985 turbocharged engines had all but taken over in Formula 1. There was a huge difference in power between the F1 cars and the accepted 'feeder' series for up-and-coming drivers, Formula 2, with its 2.0-litre production-based engines. F2 was also becoming prohibitively expensive with the appearance of highly developed 'works' engines. So for 1985, a new series, Formula 3000, replaced F2, with full-race engines of 3.0-litres capacity – the same as the now-outmoded 'atmo' F1 engines. It meant that Cosworth's DFV, which had seemed to be heading rapidly for the history books, suddenly had another new lease of life. Mandatory 9,000rpm rev limiters restricted the power output to around 450bhp, and extended the life of the engines between overhauls to reduce running costs.

Ralt, AGS and March built new cars for the new formula, while Lola adapted their existing IndyCar chassis. Some teams ran old Williams, Arrows and Tyrrell F1 cars. The 1985 European F3000 season was dominated by Mike Thackwell, Emanuele Pirro and Christian Danner, and ultimately it was Danner who won the championship in a March.

That first year had been reasonably well-supported with entries and had shown the potential of the series, and in 1986 the F3000 grids were full to capacity. For Cosworth it meant a brand-new market for DFV engines and components, at a time when its road-car engineering work was running at a higher level than ever,

and many hours were going into the GB turbo V6.

In 1986, many teams ran March 86B chassis, fitted of course, with Cosworth DFV engines. Ivan Capelli emerged as the European Champion. Cosworth's domination of the series the following year, received its first serious challenge, with the appearance of a 3.0-litre Honda V8, derived by John Judd from an IndyCar design. The Ralt-engined Hondas were fast but unlucky, and the 1987 European Champion, Stefano Modena, relied on DFV power. In the Japanese series Yamaha tried its five-valve cylinder heads on a DFV bottom end, but found that they made little difference under the mandatory 9,000rpm rev limit.

Roberto Moreno took the

new Reynard 88D chassis (with DFV engine built by Nicholson McLaren) to the European title in 1988, a season full of accidents and incidents, and Jean Alesi won in 1989 with a Reynard 89D run by Eddie Jordan. By then there was a new challenger to the DFV's supremacy, the Honda-based Mugen V8, which was torquier in the mid-range and could accelerate better out of low-speed corners. Although the DFV continued in the British F3000 Championship it was no longer competitive in the European series as the top teams started spending more and more. Cosworth were back in 1993, but with a different engine – the AC series – which dominated F3000 for three seasons before it was made obsolete by a rule change.

DFVs dominated the early years of Formula 3000, but by 1990 its place at the top had been taken by the torquey Mugen V8. At Hockenheim, Damon Hill's DFV-powered Lola started from pole position, but spun out of the race.

1989. For turbo teams like Benetton the choice was to continue with turbo engine development for one more season, knowing that the engine would be obsolete at the end of the year, or to embrace the coming 'atmo' era and hope to be reasonably competitive with the remaining turbos during 1988. Benetton chose to drop the GB turbo engine in favour of a 3.5-litre normally aspirated unit from Cosworth, but this was not the DFZ unit which the 1987 'atmo' cars had been using – instead, it was to be another new member of the DFV family.

Yamaha had designed five-valve cylinder heads, with three inlet valves and two exhausts, which could flow more air than a conventional four-valve head and would, theoretically, produce more power. The heads had been tried in Formula 3000 in Japan, but with that formula's 9,000rpm rev limit the extra air flow capability was not really required and so the five-valve heads made little difference. Under the less restrictive rules of Formula 1, however, it was thought that the Yamaha heads might help the DFZ to produce more power. Ford, which already had links with Yamaha through road-car engine development, was keen to use the Yamaha heads on the DFZ, and the hope was that they would boost the Cosworth engine from around 565bhp to 630bhp or so, at which level the Benettons would be competitive with the heavier turbo cars. Yamaha built five test engines which arrived, late, around Christmas 1987 – and on Cosworth's dynamometer they not only lacked the promised power, they struggled to keep up with a standard four-valve DFZ. Cosworth soldiered on with the five-valve head for a few more weeks, until Keith Duckworth cancelled the project in January 1988. Yamaha thought there was still potential in the idea and built its own five-valve engine which was supplied to Zakspeed in 1989, but the Zakspeed-Yamahas rarely managed to qualify and on the rare occasions they got onto the grid they didn't finish the race…

Cosworth engineer Geoff Goddard now looked in detail at every aspect of the DFZ, making hundreds of improvements. The result was called the DFR, still recognisably a DFV-series engine but with about 80 per cent new or modified components. It produced 595bhp at 11,000rpm, more than a DFZ and more than any other atmo engine, but still considerably less than the best of the turbo engines. Even so, on its debut in Brazil in Rory Byrne's Benetton B188, newcomer Alessandro Nannini was third fastest in some of the practice sessions, although he could manage no better than 12th in official qualifying. He then retired early on with his DFR overheating, a problem which also affected team-mate Thierry Boutsen who finished seventh. In the

San Marino Grand Prix both cars were slowed by cracked exhausts but finished fourth and sixth, a lap down on the leading Honda-powered trio. Monaco proved difficult (Nannini retired with gearbox problems, Boutsen finished eighth after a puncture), but the Benettons ran reliably at altitude in Mexico to finish seventh and eighth behind a gaggle of turbo cars, which could exploit their power advantage in the thin air. Boutsen was third in Canada behind the two McLaren-Hondas, and repeated the feat a week later in Detroit. Nannini's Benetton was the top 'atmo' car in France, finishing in sixth place, and at Silverstone he finished third behind Senna's winning McLaren-Honda and Mansell's Williams-Judd. In Germany, Boutsen was sixth, but Nannini had a throttle-cable bracket break while he was holding fourth position. Boutsen was third behind the two McLaren-Hondas in Hungary and again at Spa, this time with Nannini fourth, but much later the team's fuel was found to be illegal and they were disqualified from the Belgian race.

Boutsen continued his run of form, with sixth place in Italy and third in Portugal, then tangled with Capelli's March in Spain and ended up ninth while team-mate Nannini stormed through the field after a poor start to claim the bottom step of the podium. In Japan, Boutsen was third and Nannini fifth, and in the final race of the season in Australia, Boutsen finished fifth to secure fourth place in the World Drivers' Championship and third in the Constructors' Championship for Benetton-Ford behind the turbo McLaren-Hondas and Ferraris.

By the middle of 1988, Cosworth's Geoff Goddard was working on a brand-new 3.5-litre engine for the 1989 season. A V12 was considered, but ultimately the fuel consumption and packaging advantages of a V8 won the day. Taking advantage of modern design techniques and computer analysis the new engine would be a 75-degree V8, the tighter V-angle making it narrower than a DFV. It was also lower, but at least as long, suggesting that it had a wider bore and shorter stroke – although no details were released, in contrast to the wealth of information which had been provided at the launch of the DFV. The HB, as it was called, first ran in December of that year and it was officially revealed to the press in March 1989, when Ford claimed it delivered more than 600bhp – but was cagey about exact figures.

For the first few races of 1989, Benetton relied on the DFR-engined B188 while the HB-engined B189 was being developed. Nannini finished third in San Marino and fourth in Mexico, then his new team-mate

Johnny Herbert finished fifth at Phoenix. The new car made its debut in France, and at the end of the season scored a lucky win when Ayrton Senna's McLaren was disqualified. Only Benetton was supplied with the HB, while Cosworth's 'customer' teams relied on the DFR. Occasionally the DFR upset the formbook, notably at Phoenix in 1990 where Jean Alesi's Tyrrell 018 qualified fourth and led the race in the early stages, fending off Ayrton Senna, and eventually finishing second to the Brazilian – a minute ahead of Nelson Piquet in the Benetton. Tyrrell switched to Honda engines for 1991 but several other teams retained DFRs built by Mader or Brian Hart. That was the 24th and final season for the DFV-family in Formula 1.

Walter Hayes leafs through his F1 pictures from the early 1980s. The engine he had helped to bring to fruition, the DFV, was reaching the end of its long career.

UPHILL STRUGGLE: COSWORTH POWER IN HILLCLIMBING

Alister Douglas-Osborn won the British Hillclimb Championship in 1977 with a Pilbeam MP22 powered by a DFV V8. Although DFVs would regularly appear in top-level hillclimb single-seaters throughout the late 1970s and the 1980s, it was Hart turbo engines which dominated the sport until the 1990s. Once DFR engines began to percolate through from Formula 1 – where they were now outclassed – they began a more successful period for the DFV family in what is one of the most friendly branches of motorsport.

Martyn Griffiths won the championship three times with Hart power and then switched to a DFR-engined Pilbeam MP58, winning the title in 1990 and successfully defending it in 1991. In 1992 Roy Lane won the championship with an MP58 fitted with a DFL engine, then David Grace (later to become boss of the new Rockingham track in Northamptonshire) won a pair of titles in his MP58 with DFR power. In 1995 Andy Priaulx won the title with a DFV-engined MP58, but in 1996 and 1997 the title went to cars powered by Judd EV engines.

The DFR was back in 1998 with the first of three successive titles for David Grace, who had moved on from the Pilbeam to a Gould GR37. Since then, hillclimb single-seaters have moved on to smaller, lighter and more modern engines which offer similar power outputs – but the DFV family, and in particular the heavily-revised DFR in the 1990s, can look back on a successful career in hillclimbing.

FAR LEFT: *DFVs arrived on the hills in the early 1970s. One of the earliest Cosworth-powered cars was Sir Nick Williamson's Marlyn, seen at Shelsley Walsh in 1974.*

LEFT: *In 1977, Alister Douglas-Osborn became the first British Hillclimb Champion to use DFV power, in this Pilbeam MP22.*

ABOVE: *David Grace – seen here cresting Deer Leap at Gurston Down – won three successive British Hillclimb Championship titles in this DFR-engined Gould GR37.*

CHAPTER TEN

DFVs TODAY

Formula 1 has changed almost beyond recognition over the last three decades, and the technology it now employs is far beyond what most teams could even have imagined in the 1960s and '70s. Those days have gone for ever, but fortunately for enthusiasts who remember the Cosworth era, the characteristic bark of the DFV V8 can still be heard around the world's greatest racing venues. It is all thanks to the dedicated individuals and organisations which track down, restore and race old Formula 1 machinery in historic F1 championships like the FIA Thoroughbred Grand Prix series.

The TGP series caters for all 3.0-litre Formula 1 cars from 1966 to 1985. Each car must conform to the Formula 1 regulations which were in effect when it was new, and there must be evidence that it was successfully scrutineered at an international F1 event. Prototype 3.0-litre F1 cars of the period are also eligible if their provenance can be established, but turbocharged cars are not eligible. The series is particularly appealing for spectators because the cars still run in their original liveries. The rules mandate that the bodywork of each car must be of the original design, and the livery must be that used on the car during its international racing career – subject to any modern laws at certain events which ban, for instance, tobacco advertising.

No alterations may be made to the car's chassis, although appropriate repairs can be made. The suspension system must be as original, though active systems can be converted back to non-active suspension used in period. Carbon-carbon brakes are banned, and any cars fitted with them must be converted to steel discs with contemporary calipers and conventional pads.

September 2006: Thoroughbred Grand Prix competitors, most powered by DFV engines, rest between practice sessions at Donington. Ean Pugh's 'lobster claw' Brabham BT34 heads the line-up.

Wheels must be of the original diameter used during the car's international racing career. Rim widths may be decreased to accommodate the tyres which are available, but may not be increased beyond the maximum used in-period. Most of the cars race on a 'control' slick tyre, the Avon A11 cross-ply (or a standard Avon wet-weather tyre) and only one set of tyres is permitted at each meeting. Older cars may use Dunlop CR65 treaded race tyres. Tyre warming blankets are banned.

The engines in TGP cars must be of the same make and type fitted when the cars were new, and must run at the original cubic capacity. DFV-powered cars make up the bulk of the grids, although occasionally, BRM V12s, Ferrari flat-12s and other 3.0-litre engines can be heard amongst the Cosworths. Cars originally fitted with early DFVs can be fitted with later short-stroke engines, but cannot use DFYs unless there is evidence this engine was fitted in-period. The ignition system must be of a type using during the car's racing career – electronic engine management systems are specifically banned – and each engine must be limited to 10,500rpm. Electronic instrumentation may be fitted but data acquisition is limited to basic engine data.

Cars originally fitted with semi-automatic

ABOVE: *Richard Eyre's Williams FW08 in the pits at Donington in 2006. The Thoroughbred Grand Prix series attracts a wide range of cars and provides a great spectacle.*

RIGHT: *Another TGP regular, John Crowson's Ensign N177. The TGP series is restricted to non-turbo 3.0-litre grand prix cars, most of which are DFV-powered.*

transmissions may be converted to a manual gearbox, but otherwise gearboxes must be of the same type as used during the vehicle's competition history. The final drive including the differential must conform to the manufacturer's original specification.

Aerodynamic devices may only be fitted if they were used during the car's racing career, and then they must conform in design, positioning and dimensions to those used during the car's international life. No cockpit-adjustable aerodynamic devices are permitted, and wings fitted to unsprung parts of the car are banned. Cars which originally ran with aerodynamic devices may be run without. Oil coolers can be repositioned, provided that the car's silhouette is not altered. Fuel tanks must either be replaced with modern tanks, or filled with safety foam. Fire extinguisher systems of the car's original type must be fitted and working, and can be supplemented by modern systems. All cars must have a red rear warning light.

Minimum weight limits and maximum dimensions vary depending on the age of the car. Cars built or raced in 1966–1969 have a 500kg minimum, gradually increasing up to 585kg for 1981–82 cars before dropping back to 540kg for the 1983–85 cars.

All cars are subject to a minimum ground clearance of 40mm, which largely negates the advantage of the ground-effect cars. Cars that ran fixed aerodynamic skirts in-period may retain the skirt fixing, but the skirt must be modified to maintain the mandatory 40mm minimum static ground clearance. Rubbing strips are not permitted. Any device fitted to the car to lower its ground clearance while in motion – a popular ruse among F1 teams in the early '80s, to get round a mandatory minimum static ride-height – must be disabled.

The result of all these stipulations is a grid of F1 cars which look much the same as they would have done in their heyday, in addition to which cars of disparate ages can compete on a reasonably fair basis. To level the playing field still further, the cars compete in four different classes. Class A admits cars built from 1966 to 1971; Class B is for non-ground-effect cars built between 1972 and 1979; Class C caters for ground-effect cars from 1977 to 1982 and Class D includes all the flat-bottom cars from 1983 to 1985. Competition is healthy, with everything from ex-Stewart Tyrrells to 1980s McLarens and Arrows appearing in the TGP grids.

One of the best known teams in the series is Classic

John Delane's ex-Jackie Stewart Tyrrell 003 is one of the earliest cars in the TGP series.

Team Lotus run by Clive Chapman, son of Lotus founder Colin Chapman. 'My family had a collection of about 25 cars,' he says. 'They weren't really being looked after, so I hooked up with some of the original Team Lotus mechanics and started Classic Team Lotus.' The team also offers a service to other Lotus owners who want to restore and compete in their cars, without getting too involved in the minutiae of running them on a day-to-day basis. Classic Team Lotus's own cars also get used within the team's patron scheme. Preparation of the cars between races takes at least 40 hours and at race meetings Classic Team Lotus has two mechanics looking after each car. Despite the man hours involved, the costs are surprisingly affordable, says Chapman. 'A lot of people are surprised how inexpensive it can be to race a 1980s F1 car. And they are raced, they don't hang about. Some of them are matching the times that were done originally. Maybe the engines have a bit more power, maybe the tyres have a bit more grip, the circuits might be smoother. But drivers like Duncan Dayton, Joaquin Folk, Martin Stretton and Simon Hadfield are just bloody quick.'

The engine is one of the biggest difficulties of managing the use of a historic F1 car because of the cost of rebuild and repairs, says Chapman. 'It's really the engine that's the most expensive aspect of racing historic Formula 1. We tend to do it in 1,000-mile bites. The patron takes the engine over at zero miles and he takes the risk. As soon as you get one engine doing 100 miles, then someone else hops in and it blows up after one lap – "it's not my fault". So that's fundamental.'

For a while the competition in TGP led drivers to work the engines harder and harder, and costs escalated. 'Customers tend to want to get as much power as humanly possible,' says Clive Chapman with a wry grin. 'They started revving the engines in TGP up to about 11,300rpm and they had to rebuild them very regularly, which started to put people off getting involved in the series.' Engine builders were developing the DFV beyond its final F1 incarnations, with different pistons, aggressive cam profiles and higher compression ratios, and rebuilds were needed every 350 miles. To restore order a mandatory rev limit of 10,500rpm was introduced. 'The limit is simply done in the spark box. I'm sure you could get round it if you really wanted to, so you have to rely on people playing the game – which they never would have in period,' says Chapman. 'But if you start cheating in historics, that's pretty sad…'

Although the engines are reliable and there are still supplies of essential parts to keep the DFVs running, Chapman says one problem is that there are so many different specifications. 'It's important to have the spec of the engines the same,' he says. 'In the day, that was just a given, but over such a long period of time and the engines having been with so many privateer teams and engine builders, they have developed into a smorgasbord of specifications. The number of times customers have said they've got a spare engine that's exactly the same – they look at them and say "I've got two DFVs" – but we say this is different, that's different…' Engines from the ground-effect era, for example, have a different oil and water pump layout to reduce the intrusion of the pumps into the ground-effect venturis. 'The slimline pump system is much better,' says Classic Team Lotus team manager Chris Dinnage, 'but the cars that ran them in-period were designed for them. Now people are putting short stroke engines in cars which were designed for long stroke engines with the wide auxiliaries, and it becomes a bit of a plumbing nightmare on some of them.'

The problem comes when an engine change is required, because of a failure or because an engine needs to be overhauled. Differences in plumbing and throttle control make the engine change more

TGP champion in 2006, Steve Hartley, at the wheel of his Arrows A6 in practice for the Donington round of the championship where he qualified third and finished third.

LEFT: *Joquim Folch's Brabham BT49 on the way to pole position at Donington in 2006. Folch was second in the 2006 TGP championship.*

BELOW: *Rowland Kinch's Arrows A1 in its distinctive gold Warsteiner livery. The TGP cars are required to run in their original colour schemes, subject to any modern advertising regulations.*

time consuming. 'We had an engine change to do at Donington, from the morning session to the afternoon,' says Chapman. 'That was fairly straightforward because Dan Collins has had those engines for a long time, and just rotates them. They've become the same spec. We did it in four hours – Peter Warr said they used to do it in an hour and a half in his day!'

The DFVs are operated in much the same way as they were in their heyday, although now there is inevitably less emphasis on extracting every last drop of power and more on maintaining reliability and keeping costs as low as possible. Start-up from cold can cause a lot of wear, and to minimise that Classic Team Lotus fit water heaters to pre-heat the engines before starting them. 'It's something we never, ever used to do in-period, but something we've started to do in historic racing,' says Chris Dinnage. 'The engines sit around for a long period of time without being started, so it all helps. We'd plug the water heater on and warm it up to 40°C minimum – if it goes up to 70°C that's not a problem.' The fuel cam is then set to the richest of its five mixture positions. 'When the thing is cold and we start it up first thing in the morning, we start it on full rich – effectively like putting the choke on,' says Dinnage. 'The normal position is one away from full lean. In wet weather we'd

run it in the middle position, because it doesn't really lose an awful lot of horsepower by richening it up a bit but it makes it less responsive, so it's less likely to light up the rear wheels. Altitude makes a difference – when we go to places like Kyalami, we change the fuel cam.'

'If it's been started recently we'd just squirt some petrol down the trumpets and kick it into life. If it's been left a couple of months we have the plugs out, and just crank it over to make sure the oil pressure comes round, then put the plugs back in.' One important task to remember is to turn on the electric fuel pump before attempting to start the engine, then turn it off again once the engine is running. 'They've all got an electric and a mechanical fuel pump – there's lots of different sorts. You need the electrical pump to ensure the fuel injectors are running at the right pressure, but the electrical pumps can't generate enough flow to keep the engine going at high revs. The mechanical is the other way round – you can't start it up on the mechanical, and it doesn't provide enough pressure until 2,000rpm.' It is possible to leave the electric pump running all the time, says Dinnage, but there are pros and cons. 'The benefit of that is that if the driver spins he still has fuel pressure, so he has a chance of keeping the engine going. The

fairly major disadvantage is that the mechanical fuel pump is driven by the belt on the front of the engine, and if you have a belt failure the mechanical pump will stop providing fuel and it stops the engine. If you leave the electric pump on it keeps supplying fuel, so the engine keeps running – but the water pump and the oil pump aren't running…'

Classic Team Lotus runs its DFVs on 97-octane Super Unleaded fuel, adding one per cent two-stroke oil to lubricate the metering unit of the mechanical fuel injection system. The cars return around 5–6mpg in racing conditions. Some teams add octane booster additives or run on expensive 102 octane racing fuel, but Dinnage has yet to see a big advantage from that. 'We've tried it several times and we tried it again at Hockenheim this year, but it didn't make any noticeable difference to lap times and the drivers couldn't feel the difference.'

Even if there is no longer a need to extract every last horsepower, the F1 cars of the TGP championship still provide all the spectacle of Formula 1 racing in what many consider to be its golden era. Certainly for ex-mechanics like Chris Dinnage the passing of the DFV marked the end of an era in F1 racing. 'They're one

of the last engines, if not the last engine, in F1 that a decent race mechanic could understand and repair. A good mechanic can try to get the thing on the road again,' he says. Others have their own reasons for remembering this most successful of engines fondly. 'I think one of the excitements of Formula 1 was the different tones of engine,' says 1979 World Champion Jody Scheckter. 'That added a lot to Formula 1. Today, every car sounds the same, and that's quite sad.' The tight regulation of engine type, he says, also limits the excitement generated by innovation and different engineering solutions – Scheckter, remember, raced in an era when V8s, V12s, flat-12s and turbo V6s were all competitive. 'The race of technology was as exciting as the race on the track,' he says.

At Williams, Patrick Head is in no doubt about the DFV's significance for him and the Grove team. 'I think it was brilliant for F1. Without that engine, this company would not be in existence.' But it's the company's founder and figurehead, Sir Frank Williams, who perhaps sums up the DFV's contribution to Formula 1 most succinctly: 'It was an outstanding piece of equipment. It was a very neat, carefully thought-through package – and it ran like a train most of the time.'

ABOVE: *The starting procedure for DFVs is the same now as it was when they were new, though some teams like to pre-heat the engines to minimise wear during start-up. This is a McLaren M23 at the Goodwood Festival of Speed in 2003.*

LEFT: *DFVs, like any racing engines, can sometimes be moody and a little extra effort has to be employed to get them to start. Classic Team Lotus put its back into the job on a Lotus 79, dodging the spectators in the Goodwood Festival of Speed paddock.*

APPENDICES

APPENDIX A: FORMULA 1 RACE WINS

Formula 1 World Championship race wins 1967–83 – Cosworth DFV and DFY

Abbreviations: FL fastest lap, PP pole position

1967

	Race	Circuit	Date	Driver	Car	
1	Dutch GP	Zandvoort	4.6.67	J. Clark	Lotus 49	FL
2	British GP	Silverstone	15.7.67	J. Clark	Lotus 49	FL PP
3	US GP	Watkins Glen	1.10.67	J. Clark	Lotus 49	
4	Mexican GP	Mexico City	22.10.67	J. Clark	Lotus 49	FL

1968

	Race	Circuit	Date	Driver	Car	
5	South African GP	Kyalami	1.1.68	J. Clark	Lotus 49	FL
6	Spanish GP	Járama	12.5.68	G. Hill	Lotus 49	
7	Monaco GP	Monte Carlo	26.5.68	G. Hill	Lotus 49B	PP
8	Belgian GP	Spa	9.6.68	B. McLaren	McLaren M7A	
9	Dutch GP	Zandvoort	23.6.68	J. Stewart	Matra MS10	
10	British GP	Brands Hatch	20.7.68	J. Siffert	Lotus 49B	FL
11	German GP	Nürburgring	4.8.68	J. Stewart	Matra MS10	FL
12	Italian GP	Monza	8.9.68	D. Hulme	McLaren M7A	
13	Canadian GP	Mont-Tremblant	22.9.68	D. Hulme	McLaren M7A	
14	US GP	Watkins Glen	6.10.68	J. Stewart	Matra MS10	FL
15	Mexican GP	Mexico City	3.11.68	G. Hill	Lotus 49B	

1969

	Race	Circuit	Date	Driver	Car	
16	South African GP	Kyalami	1.3.69	J. Stewart	Matra MS10	FL
17	Spanish GP	Jarama	4.5.69	J. Stewart	Matra MS10	
18	Monaco GP	Monte Carlo	18.5.69	G. Hill	Lotus 49B	
19	Dutch GP	Zandvoort	21.6.69	J. Stewart	Matra MS80	FL
20	French GP	Clermont-Ferrand	6.7.69	J. Stewart	Matra MS80	FL
21	British GP	Silverstone	19.7.69	J. Stewart	Matra MS80	FL
22	German GP	Nürburgring	3.8.69	J. Ickx	Brabham BT26A	FL PP
23	Italian GP	Monza	7.9.69	J. Stewart	Matra MS80	
24	Canadian GP	Mosport Park	20.9.69	J. Ickx	Brabham BT26A	FL PP
25	US GP	Watkins Glen	5.10.69	J. Rindt	Lotus 49B	FL PP
26	Mexican GP	Mexico City	19.10.69	D. Hulme	McLaren M7A	

1970

	Race	Circuit	Date	Driver	Car	
27	South African GP	Kyalami	7.3.70	J. Brabham	Brabham BT33	FL
28	Spanish GP	Járama	19.4.70	J. Stewart	March 701	
29	Monaco GP	Monte Carlo	10.5.70	J. Rindt	Lotus 49C	
30	Dutch GP	Zandvoort	21.6.70	J. Rindt	Lotus 72C	PP
31	French GP	Clermont-Ferrand	5.7.70	J. Rindt	Lotus 72C	
32	British GP	Brands Hatch	18.7.70	J. Rindt	Lotus 72C	PP
33	German GP	Nürburgring	2.8.70	J. Rindt	Lotus 72C	
34	US GP	Watkins Glen	4.10.70	E. Fittipaldi	Lotus 72C	

1971

	Race	Circuit	Date	Driver	Car	
35	Spanish GP	Montjuic Park	18.4.71	J. Stewart	Tyrrell 003	
36	Monaco GP	Monte Carlo	23.5.71	J. Stewart	Tyrrell 003	FL PP
37	French GP	Paul Ricard	4.7.71	J. Stewart	Tyrrell 003	FL PP
38	British GP	Silverstone	17.7.71	J. Stewart	Tyrrell 003	FL
39	German GP	Nürburgring	1.8.71	J. Stewart	Tyrrell 003	PP
40	Canadian GP	Mosport Park	19.9.71	J. Stewart	Tyrrell 003	PP
41	US GP	Watkins Glen	3.10.71	F. Cevert	Tyrrell 002	

1972

	Race	Circuit	Date	Driver	Car	
42	Argentine GP	Buenos Aires	23.1.72	J. Stewart	Tyrrell 003	FL
43	South African GP	Kyalami	4.3.72	D. Hulme	McLaren M19A	
44	Spanish GP	Járama	1.5.72	E. Fittipaldi	Lotus 72D	
45	Belgian GP	Nivelles-Baulers	4.6.72	E. Fittipaldi	Lotus 72D	PP
46	French GP	Clermont-Ferrand	2.7.72	J. Stewart	Tyrrell 003	
47	British GP	Brands Hatch	15.7.72	E. Fittipaldi	Lotus 72D	
48	Austrian GP	Österreichring	13.8.72	E. Fittipaldi	Lotus 72D	PP
49	Italian GP	Monza	10.9.72	E. Fittipaldi	Lotus 72D	
50	Canadian GP	Mosport Park	24.9.72	J. Stewart	Tyrrell 005	FL
51	US GP	Watkins Glen	8.10.72	J. Stewart	Tyrrell 005	FL PP

1973

	Race	Circuit	Date	Driver	Car	
52	Argentine GP	Buenos Aires	28.1.73	E. Fittipaldi	Lotus 72D	FL
53	Brazilian GP	Interlagos	11.2.73	E. Fittipaldi	Lotus 72D	FL
54	South African GP	Kyalami	3.3.73	J. Stewart	Tyrrell 006	
55	Spanish GP	Montjuic Park	29.4.73	E. Fittipaldi	Lotus 72D	
56	Belgian GP	Zolder	20.5.73	J. Stewart	Tyrrell 006	
57	Monaco GP	Monte Carlo	3.6.73	J. Stewart	Tyrrell 006	PP
58	Swedish GP	Anderstorp	17.6.73	D. Hulme	McLaren M23	FL
59	French GP	Paul Ricard	1.7.73	R. Peterson	Lotus 72E	
60	British GP	Silverstone	14.7.73	P. Revson	McLaren M23	
61	Dutch GP	Zandvoort	29.7.73	J. Stewart	Tyrrell 006	
62	German GP	Nürburgring	5.8.73	J. Stewart	Tyrrell 006	PP
63	Austrian GP	Österreichring	19.8.73	R. Peterson	Lotus 72E	
64	Italian GP	Monza	9.9.73	R. Peterson	Lotus 72E	PP
65	Canadian GP	Mosport Park	23.9.73	P. Revson	McLaren M23	
66	US GP	Watkins Glen	7.10.73	R. Peterson	Lotus 72E	PP

1974

	Race	Circuit	Date	Driver	Car	
67	Argentine GP	Buenos Aires	13.1.74	D. Hulme	McLaren M23	
68	Brazilian GP	Interlagos	27.1.74	E. Fittipaldi	McLaren M23	PP
69	South African GP	Kyalami	30.3.74	C. Reutemann	Brabham BT44	FL
70	Belgian GP	Nivelles-Baulers	12.5.74	E. Fittipaldi	McLaren M23	
71	Monaco GP	Monte Carlo	26.5.74	R. Peterson	Lotus 72E	FL
72	Swedish GP	Anderstorp	9.6.74	J. Scheckter	Tyrrell 007	
73	French GP	Dijon-Prenois	7.7.74	R. Peterson	Lotus 72E	
74	British GP	Brands Hatch	20.7.74	J. Scheckter	Tyrrell 007	
75	Austrian GP	Österreichring	18.8.74	C. Reutemann	Brabham BT44	
76	Italian GP	Monza	8.9.74	R. Peterson	Lotus 72E	
77	Canadian GP	Mosport Park	22.9.74	E. Fittipaldi	McLaren M23	PP
78	US GP	Watkins Glen	6.10.74	C. Reutemann	Brabham BT44	PP

1975

	Race	Circuit	Date	Driver	Car
79	Argentine GP	Buenos Aires	12.1.75	E. Fittipaldi	McLaren M23

80	Brazilian GP	Interlagos	26.1.75	C. Pace	Brabham BT44B	
81	South African GP	Kyalami	1.3.75	J. Scheckter	Tyrrell 007	
82	Spanish GP	Montjuic Park	27.4.75	J. Mass	McLaren M23	
83	Dutch GP	Zandvoort	22.6.75	J. Hunt	Hesketh 308	
84	British GP	Silverstone	19.7.75	E. Fittipaldi	McLaren M23	
85	German GP	Nürburgring	3.8.75	C. Reutemann	Brabham BT44B	
86	Austrian GP	Österreichring	17.8.75	V. Brambilla	March 751	FL

1976

	Race	Circuit	Date	Driver	Car	
87	Spanish GP	Járama	2.5.76	J. Hunt	McLaren M23	PP
88	Swedish GP	Anderstorp	13.6.76	J. Scheckter	Tyrrell P34	PP
89	French GP	Paul Ricard	4.7.76	J. Hunt	McLaren M23	PP
90	German GP	Nürburgring	1.8.76	J. Hunt	McLaren M23	PP
91	Austrian GP	Österreichring	15.8.76	J. Watson	Penske PC4	
92	Dutch GP	Zandvoort	29.8.76	J. Hunt	McLaren M23	
93	Italian GP	Monza	12.9.76	R. Peterson	March 761	FL
94	Canadian GP	Mosport Park	3.10.76	J. Hunt	McLaren M23	PP
95	US GP (East)	Watkins Glen	10.10.76	J. Hunt	McLaren M23	FL PP
96	Japanese GP	Fuji	24.10.76	M. Andretti	Lotus 77	PP

1977

	Race	Circuit	Date	Driver	Car	
97	Argentine GP	Buenos Aires	9.1.77	J. Scheckter	Wolf WR1	
98	US GP (West)	Watkins Glen	3.4.77	M. Andretti	Lotus 78	
99	Spanish GP	Járama	8.5.77	M. Andretti	Lotus 78	PP
100	Monaco GP	Monte Carlo	22.5.77	J. Scheckter	Wolf WR1	FL
101	Belgian GP	Zolder	5.6.77	G. Nilsson	Lotus 78	FL
102	French GP	Dijon-Prenois	3.7.77	M. Andretti	Lotus 78	FL PP
103	British GP	Silverstone	16.7.77	J. Hunt	McLaren M26	FL PP
104	Austrian GP	Österreichring	14.8.77	A. Jones	Shadow DN8	
105	Italian GP	Monza	11.9.77	M. Andretti	Lotus 78	FL
106	US GP (East)	Watkins Glen	2.10.77	J. Hunt	McLaren M26	PP
107	Canadian GP	Mosport Park	9.10.77	J. Scheckter	Wolf WR1	
108	Japanese GP	Fuji	23.10.77	J. Hunt	McLaren M26	

1978

	Race	Circuit	Date	Driver	Car	
109	Argentine GP	Buenos Aires	15.1.78	M. Andretti	Lotus 78	PP
110	South African GP	Kyalami	4.3.78	R. Peterson	Lotus 78	
111	Monaco GP	Monte Carlo	7.5.78	P. Depailler	Tyrrell 008	
112	Belgian GP	Zolder	21.5.78	M. Andretti	Lotus 79	PP
113	Spanish GP	Járama	4.6.78	M. Andretti	Lotus 79	FL PP
114	French GP	Paul Ricard	2.7.78	M. Andretti	Lotus 79	
115	German GP	Hockenheim	30.7.78	M. Andretti	Lotus 79	PP
116	Austrian GP	Österreichring	13.8.78	R. Peterson	Lotus 79	FL PP
117	Dutch GP	Zandvoort	27.8.78	M. Andretti	Lotus 79	PP

1979

	Race	Circuit	Date	Driver	Car	
118	Argentine GP	Buenos Aires	21.1.79	J. Laffite	Ligier JS11	FL PP
119	Brazilian GP	Interlagos	4.2.79	J. Laffite	Ligier JS11	FL PP
120	Spanish GP	Járama	29.4.79	P. Depailler	Ligier JS11	
121	British GP	Silverstone	14.7.79	G. Regazzoni	Williams FW07	FL
122	German GP	Hockenheim	29.7.79	A. Jones	Williams FW07	
123	Austrian GP	Österreichring	12.8.79	A. Jones	Williams FW07	
124	Dutch GP	Zandvoort	26.8.79	A. Jones	Williams FW07	
125	Canadian GP	Montreal	30.9.79	A. Jones	Williams FW07	FL PP

1980

	Race	Circuit	Date	Driver	Car	
126	Argentine GP	Buenos Aires	13.1.80	A. Jones	Williams FW07	FL PP
127	US GP (West)	Long Beach	30.3.80	N. Piquet	Brabham BT49	FL PP
128	Belgian GP	Zolder	4.5.80	D. Pironi	Ligier JS11/15	
129	Monaco GP	Monte Carlo	18.5.80	C. Reutemann	Williams FW07B	FL
130	French GP	Paul Ricard	29.6.80	A. Jones	Williams FW07B	FL
131	British GP	Brands Hatch	13.7.80	A. Jones	Williams FW07B	
132	German GP	Hockenheim	10.8.80	J. Laffite	Ligier JS11/15	
133	Dutch GP	Zandvoort	31.8.80	N. Piquet	Brabham BT49	
134	Italian GP	Imola	14.9.80	N. Piquet	Brabham BT49	
135	Canadian GP	Montreal	28.9.80	A. Jones	Williams FW07B	
136	US GP (East)	Watkins Glen	5.10.80	A. Jones	Williams FW07B	FL

1981

	Race	Circuit	Date	Driver	Car	
137	US GP (West)	Long Beach	15.3.81	A. Jones	Williams FW07C	FL
138	Brazilian GP	Rio de Janeiro	29.3.81	C. Reutemann	Williams FW07C	
139	Argentine GP	Buenos Aires	12.4.81	N. Piquet	Brabham BT49C	FL PP
140	San Marino GP	Imola	3.5.81	N. Piquet	Brabham BT49C	
141	Belgian GP	Zolder	17.5.81	C. Reutemann	Williams FW07C	FL PP
142	British GP	Silverstone	18.7.81	J. Watson	McLaren MP4	
143	German GP	Hockenheim	2.8.81	N. Piquet	Brabham BT49C	
144	Caesar's Palace GP	Las Vegas	17.10.81	A. Jones	Williams FW07C	

1982

	Race	Circuit	Date	Driver	Car	
145	US GP (West)	Long Beach	4.4.82	N. Lauda	McLaren MP4B	FL
146	Belgian GP	Zolder	9.5.82	J. Watson	McLaren MP4B	FL
147	Monaco GP	Monte Carlo	23.5.82	R. Patrese	Brabham BT49D	FL
148	US GP	Detroit	6.6.82	J. Watson	McLaren MP4B	
149	British GP	Brands Hatch	18.7.82	N. Lauda	McLaren MP4B	
150	Austrian GP	Österreichring	15.8.82	E. de Angelis	Lotus 91	
151	Swiss GP	Dijon-Prenois	29.8.82	K. Rosberg	Williams FW08	
152	Caesar's Palace GP	Las Vegas	25.9.82	M. Alboreto	Tyrrell 011	FL

1983

	Race	Circuit	Date	Driver	Car	
153	US GP (West)	Long Beach	27.3.83	J. Watson	McLaren MP4/1C	
154	Monaco GP	Monte Carlo	15.5.83	K. Rosberg	Williams FW08	
155	US GP	Detroit	5.6.83	M. Alboreto	Tyrrell 011	

Non-championship F1 races

Wins in significant F1 races which were not part of the World Championship series. There were also many other non-championship F1 events and national series in South Africa and the UK.

Race of Champions

Circuit	Date	Driver	Car
Brands Hatch	17.3.68	B. McLaren	McLaren M7A
Brands Hatch	17.3.69	J. Stewart	Matra MS80
Brands Hatch	23.3.70	J. Stewart	March 701
Brands Hatch	19.3.72	E. Fittipaldi	Lotus 72
Brands Hatch	17.3.74	J. Ickx	Lotus 72
Brands Hatch	16.3.75	T. Pryce	Shadow DN5
Brands Hatch	14.3.76	J. Hunt	McLaren M23
Brands Hatch	20.3.77	J. Hunt	McLaren M23
Brands Hatch	10.4.83	K. Rosberg	Williams FW08C

BRDC International Trophy

Circuit	Date	Driver	Car
Silverstone	25.4.68	D. Hulme	McLaren M7A
Silverstone	30.3.69	J. Brabham	Brabham BT26A
Silverstone	26.4.70	C. Amon	March 701
Silverstone	8.5.71	J. Stewart	Tyrrell 003
Silverstone	23.4.72	E. Fittipaldi	Lotus 72
Silverstone	8.4.73	J. Stewart	Tyrrell 006
Silverstone	7.4.74	J. Hunt	Hesketh 308
Silverstone	11.4.76	J. Hunt	McLaren M23
Silverstone	19.3.78	K. Rosberg	Theodore TR1

International Gold Cup

Circuit	Date	Driver	Car
Oulton Park	17.8.68	J. Stewart	Matra MS10
Oulton Park	16.8.69	J. Ickx	Brabham BT26A
Oulton Park	22.8.70	J. Surtees	Surtees TS7
Oulton Park	22.8.71	H. Pescarolo	March 711
Oulton Park	29.5.72	D. Hulme	McLaren M19A

Others

Race	Date	Driver	Car
Rothmans 50,000, Brands Hatch	28.8.72	E. Fittipaldi	Lotus 72
Gunnar Nilsson Memorial Trophy, Donington	3.6.79	A. Jones	Williams FW07
Spanish Grand Prix, Jarama	1.6.80	A. Jones	Williams FW07B
South African Grand Prix, Kyalami	7.2.81	C. Reutemann	Williams FW07B

F1 statistics, records and trivia

Throughout this section, 'DFV' includes both DFV and DFY engines. All statistics apply to the 3.0-litre Formula 1 World Championship of 1966-85, except where specified.

Race entries: 267

Wins: 155 (more than 58 per cent of those entered). Over the 1966–85 period the next most successful engine manufacturer was Ferrari, with 54 wins split between V12, flat-12 and turbo V6 engines.

World Champion drivers – Nine drivers won 12 championships: Graham Hill (1968), Jackie Stewart (1969, 1971, 1973), Jochen Rindt (1970), Emerson Fittipaldi (1972, 1974), James Hunt (1976), Mario Andretti (1978), Alan Jones (1980), Nelson Piquet (1981) and Keke Rosberg (1982).

World Champion constructors – Five constructors won ten championships: Lotus (1968, 1970, 1972, 1973, 1978), Matra (1969), Tyrrell (1971), McLaren (1974) and Williams (1980, 1981). World Championship points: 3,433. The closest rival was Ferrari, with 1,051 points over the 1966–85 period.

Most dominant seasons: DFVs won all 15 races in 1973. Highest points scores were 300 in 1980, and 286 in 1973. The 1973 score was 92 per cent of the 310 points scored by all engines.

Best race and track records: DFV-powered cars won 14 British Grands Prix, eight of them at Silverstone and six at Brands Hatch. The DFVs most successful tracks were at Watkins Glen and Monaco. It won 11 GPs at each venue.

Most successful DFV-powered drivers: Jackie Stewart won 25 Grands Prix with DFV power, almost twice as many as his nearest rival, Emerson Fittipaldi (14 wins). Stewart also won Grands Prix with DFV power in six different seasons, the most of any driver. But Carlos Reutemann's seven DFV-powered victories came over a longer period, between 1974 and 1981.

Most successful DFV-powered constructors: Lotus won 47 races with DFV power, McLaren 30 and Tyrrell 23. Lotus and McLaren both had winning careers spanning 16 seasons and both won races in 11 of those seasons.

Most successful DFV-powered cars: The several incarnations of the Lotus 72 won 20 Grands Prix, followed by the McLaren M23 with 16 wins and the Williams FW07 with 15.

Longest winning run by DFV engined cars: DFVs won races every season from 1967 to 1983. The longest unbroken run of wins by the DFV was 22 races from Italy 1972 to South Africa 1974.

Most DFV entries in a single race: Belgian Grand Prix, 1974. There were 26 Cosworth DFV-powered cars on the grid, plus a Surtees which failed to qualify.

Race domination: All 16 finishers in the 1973 German Grand Prix were DFV powered. The last non-DFV challenger, Clay Regazzoni's BRM, dropped out at half distance.

_____ APPENDIX B: TASMAN _____ SERIES RACE WINS

Cosworth DFW

1968

	Race	Circuit	Date	Driver	Car
1	Lady Wigram Trophy	Wigram	20.1.68	J. Clark	Lotus 49T
2	Rothmans 100	Surfers Paradise	11.2.68	J. Clark	Lotus 49T
3	Sydney Trophy	Warwick Farm	18.2.68	J. Clark	Lotus 49T
4	Australian GP	Sandown	25.2.68	J. Clark	Lotus 49T

1969

	Race	Circuit	Date	Driver	Car
5	Lady Wigram Trophy	Wigram	19.1.69	J. Rindt	Lotus 49T
6	Teretonga International	Teretonga	25.1.69	P. Courage	Brabham BT24
7	International 100	Warwick Farm	9.2.69	J. Rindt	Lotus 49T

_____ APPENDIX C: SPORTS _____ CAR RACE WINS

International sports car race wins 1973–82 – Cosworth DFV and DFL

Includes World Sports Car Championship, World Endurance Championship races and Le Mans 24-hour races

	Race	Date	Drivers	Car
1	Spa 1,000km	6.5.73	D. Bell/M. Hailwood	Mirage M6
2	Le Mans 24-hours	15.6.75	J. Ickx/D. Bell	Gulf GR8
3	Monza 1,000km	27.4.80	A. de Cadenet/Wilson	de Cadenet Lola LM
4	Silverstone 6 hours	11.5.80	A. de Cadenet/Wilson	de Cadenet Lola LM
5	Le Mans 24-hours	15.6.80	J. Rondeau/J.-P. Jaussaud	Rondeau M379B
6	Coppa Florio	28.6.81	E. de Villota/G. Edwards	Lola T600
7	Brands Hatch 1,000km	27.9.81	E. de Villota/G. Edwards	Lola T600
8	Monza 1,000km	18.4.82	H. Pescarolo/G. Francia	Rondeau M382

Drivers Bell, de Cadenet, Wilson, de Villota and Edwards all won two races with Cosworth power. Lola is the most successful constructor with four wins.

USAC and CART wins – Cosworth DFX and DFS

1976

	Race	Date	Series	Driver	Car
1	Pocono	27.6.76	USAC	A. Unser	Parnelli
2	Milwaukee	22.8.76	USAC	A. Unser	Parnelli
3	Phoenix	7.11.76	USAC	A. Unser	Parnelli

1977

	Race	Date	Series	Driver	Car
4	Phoenix	27.3.77	USAC	J. Rutherford	McLaren
5	Texas World	2.4.77	USAC	T. Sneva	McLaren
6	Milwaukee	12.6.77	USAC	J. Rutherford	McLaren
7	Pocono	26.6.77	USAC	T. Sneva	McLaren
8	Michigan	17.7.77	USAC	D. Ongais	Parnelli
9	Texas World	31.7.77	USAC	J. Rutherford	McLaren
10	Milwaukee	21.8.77	USAC	J. Rutherford	McLaren
11	Ontario	4.9.77	USAC	A. Unser	Parnelli

1978

	Race	Date	Series	Driver	Car
12	Ontario	26.3.78	USAC	D. Ongais	Parnelli
13	Texas World	15.4.78	USAC	D. Ongais	Parnelli
14	Indianapolis	28.5.78	USAC	A. Unser	Lola
15	Mosport Park	11.6.78	USAC	D. Ongais	Parnelli
16	Milwaukee	18.6.76	USAC	R. Mears	Penske
17	Pocono	25.6.78	USAC	A. Unser	Lola
18	Michigan	16.7.78	USAC	J. Rutherford	McLaren
19	Atlanta	23.7.78	USAC	R. Mears	Penske
20	Milwaukee	20.8.78	USAC	D. Ongais	Parnelli
21	Ontario	3.9.78	USAC	A. Unser	Lola
22	Michigan	16.9.78	USAC	D. Ongais	Parnelli
23	Trenton	23.9.78	USAC	Ma. Andretti	Penske
24	Brands Hatch	7.10.78	USAC	R. Mears	Penske
25	Phoenix	28.10.78	USAC	J. Rutherford	McLaren

1979

	Race	Date	Series	Driver	Car
26	Ontario	25.3.79	USAC	A. J. Foyt	Parnelli
27	Texas World	8.4.79	USAC	A. J. Foyt	Parnelli
28	Atlanta	22.4.79	CART	J. Rutherford	McLaren
29	Atlanta	22.4.79	CART	J. Rutherford	McLaren
30	Indianapolis	28.5.79	USAC	R. Mears	Penske
31	Milwaukee	10.6.79	USAC	A. J. Foyt	Parnelli
32	Trenton	10.6.79	CART	B. Unser	Penske
33	Trenton	10.6.79	CART	B. Unser	Penske
34	Pocono	24.6.79	USAC	A.J. Foyt	Parnelli
35	Brooklyn	15.7.79	CART	G. Johncock	Patrick Racing Penske
36	Brooklyn	15.7.79	CART	B. Unser	Penske
37	Texas World	29.7.79	USAC	A. J. Foyt	Parnelli
38	Watkins Glen	5.8.79	CART	B. Unser	Penske
39	Milwaukee	12.8.79	USAC	R. McCluskey	Lola
40	Trenton	19.8.79	CART	R. Mears	Penske
41	Ontario	2.9.79	CART	B. Unser	Penske
42	Brooklyn	15.9.79	CART	B. Unser	Penske
43	Atlanta	30.9.79	CART	R. Mears	Penske
44	Phoenix	20.10.79	CART	A. Unser	Chaparral Lola

1980

	Race	Date	Series	Driver	Car
45	Ontario	13.4.80	CART/USAC	J. Rutherford	Chaparral
46	Indianapolis	26.5.80	CART/USAC	J. Rutherford	Chaparral
47	Milwaukee	8.6.80	CART/USAC	B. Unser	Penske
48	Pocono	22.6.80	CART/USAC	B. Unser	Penske
49	Lexington	13.7.80	CART/USAC	J. Rutherford	Chaparral
50	Brooklyn	20.7.80	CART	J. Rutherford	Chaparral
51	Watkins Glen	3.8.80	CART	B. Unser	Penske
52	Milwaukee	10.8.80	CART	J. Rutherford	Chaparral
53	Ontario	31.8.80	CART	B. Unser	Penske
54	Brooklyn	20.9.80	CART	Ma. Andretti	Penske
55	Mexico City	26.10.80	CART	R. Mears	Penske
56	Phoenix	8.11.80	CART	T. Sneva	O'Connell Phoenix

1981

	Race	Date	Series	Driver	Car
57	Phoenix	22.3.81	CART	J. Rutherford	Chaparral
58	Indianapolis	24.4.81	USAC	B. Unser	Penske
59	Atlanta	21.6.81	CART	R. Mears	Penske
60	Atlanta	21.6.81	CART	R. Mears	Penske
61	Pocono	22.6.81	USAC	A.J. Foyt	March
62	Brooklyn	25.7.81	CART	P. Carter	Morales Penske
63	Riverside	30.8.81	CART	R. Mears	Penske
64	Milwaukee	5.9.81	CART	T. Sneva	Bignotti-Cotter Phoenix
65	Brooklyn	20.9.81	CART	R. Mears	Penske
66	Watkins Glen	4.10.81	CART	R. Mears	Penske
67	Mexico City	18.10.81	CART	R. Mears	Penske
68	Phoenix	31.10.81	CART	T. Sneva	Bignotti-Cotter March

1982

	Race	Date	Series	Driver	Car
69	Phoenix	28.3.82	CART	R. Mears	Penske
70	Atlanta	1.5.82	CART	R. Mears	Penske
71	Indianapolis	30.5.82	USAC	G. Johncock	Patrick Racing Wildcat
72	Milwaukee	13.6.82	CART	G. Johncock	Patrick Racing Wildcat
73	Cleveland	4.7.82	CART	B. Rahal	Truesports March
74	Brooklyn	18.7.82	CART	G. Johncock	Patric Racing Wildcat
75	Milwaukee	1.8.82	CART	T. Sneva	Bignotti-Cotter March
76	Pocono	15.8.82	CART	R. Mears	Penske
77	Riverside	29.8.82	CART	R. Mears	Penske
78	Elkhart Lake	19.9.82	CART	H. Rebaque	Forsythe March
79	Brooklyn	26.9.82	CART	B. Rahal	Truesports March
80	Phoenix	6.11.82	CART	T. Sneva	Bignotti-Cotter March

1983

	Race	Date	Series	Driver	Car
81	Atlanta	17.4.83	CART	G. Johncock	Patrick Racing Wildcat
82	Indianapolis	29.5.83	CART	T. Sneva	Bignotti-Cotter March
83	Milwaukee	12.6.83	CART	T. Sneva	Bignotti-Cotter March
84	Cleveland	3.7.83	CART	A. Unser	Penske
85	Brooklyn	17.7.83	CART	J. Paul Jnr	VDS Penske
86	Elkhart Lake	31.7.83	CART	Ma. Andretti	Newman-Haas Lola
87	Pocono	14.8.83	CART	T. Fabi	Forsythe March
88	Riverside	28.8.83	CART	B. Rahal	Truesports March
89	Lexington	11.9.83	CART	T. Fabi	Forsythe March
90	Brooklyn	18.9.83	CART	R. Mears	Penske
91	Las Vegas	8.10.83	CART	Ma. Andretti	Newman-Haas Lola
92	Monterey	23.10.83	CART	T. Fabi	Forsythe March
93	Phoenix	29.10.83	CART	T. Fabi	Forsythe March

1984

	Race	Date	Series	Driver	Car
94	Long Beach	31.3.84	CART	Ma. Andretti	Newman-Haas Lola
95	Phoenix	14.4.84	CART	T. Sneva	Mayer March
96	Indianapolis	27.5.84	CART	R. Mears	Penske March
97	Milwaukee	3.6.84	CART	T. Sneva	Mayer March
98	Portland	17.6.84	CART	A. Unser Jnr	Galles March
99	Meadowlands	1.7.84	CART	Ma. Andretti	Newman-Haas Lola
100	Cleveland	8.7.84	CART	D. Sullivan	Shierson Lola
101	Brooklyn	22.7.84	CART	Ma. Andretti	Newman-Haas Lola
102	Elkhart Lake	5.8.84	CART	Ma. Andretti	Newman-Haas Lola
103	Pocono	19.8.84	CART	D. Sullivan	Shierson Lola
104	Lexington	2.9.84	CART	Ma. Andretti	Newman-Haas Lola
105	Sanair	9.9.84	CART	D. Sullivan	Shierson Lola
106	Brooklyn	24.9.84	CART	Ma. Andretti	Newman-Haas Lola
107	Phoenix	13.10.84	CART	B. Rahal	Truesports March
108	Monterey	20.10.84	CART	B. Rahal	Truesports March
109	Las Vegas	10.11.84	CART	T. Sneva	Mayer March

1985

	Race	Date	Series	Driver	Car
110	Long Beach	14.4.85	CART	Ma. Andretti	Newman-Haas Lola
111	Indianapolis	25.5.85	CART	D. Sullivan	Penske March
112	Milwaukee	2.6.85	CART	Ma. Andretti	Newman-Haas Lola
113	Portland	16.6.85	CART	Ma. Andretti	Newman-Haas Lola
114	Meadowlands	30.6.85	CART	A. Unser Jnr	Shierson Lola
115	Cleveland	7.7.85	CART	A. Unser Jnr	Shierson Lola
116	Brooklyn	28.7.85	CART	E. Fittipaldi	Patrick Racing March
117	Elkhart Lake	4.8.85	CART	J. Villeneuve	Canadian Tire March
118	Pocono	18.8.85	CART	R. Mears	Penske March
119	Lexington	1.9.85	CART	B. Rahal	Trusports March
120	Sanair	8.9.85	CART	J. Rutherford	Morales March
121	Brooklyn	22.9.85	CART	B. Rahal	Truesports March
122	Monterey	6.10.85	CART	B. Rahal	Truesports March
123	Phoenix	13.10.85	CART	A. Unser	Penske March
124	Miami	10.11.85	CART	D. Sullivan	Penske March

1986

	Race	Date	Series	Driver	Car
125	Phoenix	5.4.86	CART	K. Cogan	Patrick Racing March
126	Long Beach	12.4.86	CART	Mi. Andretti	Kraco March
127	Indianapolis	1.6.86	CART	B. Rahal	Truesports March
128	Milwaukee	8.6.86	CART	Mi. Andretti	Kraco March
129	Portland	15.6.86	CART	Ma. Andretti	Newman-Haas Lola
130	Meadowlands	29.6.86	CART	D. Sullivan	Penske March
131	Cleveland	6.7.86	CART	D. Sullivan	Penske March
132	Toronto	20.7.86	CART	B. Rahal	Truesports March
133	Brooklyn	2.8.86	CART	J. Rutherford	Morales March
134	Pocono	17.8.86	CART	Ma. Andretti	Newman-Haas Lola
135	Lexington	31.8.86	CART	B. Rahal	Truesports March
136	Sanair	7.9.86	CART	B. Rahal	Truesports March
137	Brooklyn	28.9.86	CART	B. Rahal	Truesports March
138	Elkhart Lake	4.10.86	CART	E. Fittipaldi	Patrick Racing March
139	Monterey	12.10.86	CART	B. Rahal	Truesports March
140	Phoenix	19.10.86	CART	Mi. Andretti	Kraco March
141	Miami	9.11.86	CART	A. Unser Jnr	Shierson Lola

1987

	Race	Date	Series	Driver	Car
142	Phoenix	12.4.87	CART	R. Guerrero	Granatelli March
143	Indianapolis	31.5.87	CART	A. Unser	Penske March
144	Milwaukee	7.6.87	CART	Mi. Andretti	Kraco March
145	Portland	14.6.87	CART	B. Rahal	Truesports Lola
146	Meadowlands	28.6.87	CART	B. Rahal	Truesports Lola
147	Brooklyn	2.8.87	CART	Mi. Andretti	Kraco March
148	Lexington	6.9.87	CART	R. Guerrero	Granatelli March
149	Nazareth	20.9.87	CART	Mi. Andretti	Kraco March
150	Monterey	11.10.87	CART	B. Rahal	Truesports Lola
151	Miami	1.11.87	CART	Mi. Andretti	Kraco March

1989

	Race	Date	Series	Driver	Car
152	Meadowlands	16.7.89	CART	B. Rahal	Kraco Lola

IndyCar statistics

Wins: 152 in championship and Indy 500 races.

Champion drivers: Cosworth engines have powered seven IndyCar drivers to 12 championship wins: Tom Sneva (1977, 1978), A. J. Foyt (1979 USAC), Rick Mears (1979 CART, 1981, 1982), Johnny Rutherford (1980), Al Unser (1983, 1985), Mario Andretti (1984) and Bobby Rahal (1986, 1987).

Most successful drivers: Rick Mears (20 wins), Bobby Rahal (18), Johnny Rutherford (16), Mario Andretti (15), Tom Sneva (12), Al Unser (11) and Bobby Unser (11).

Most successful chassis constructors: March won 52 races using the Cosworth DFX engine, followed by Penske (35), Lola (28), Parnelli (15), McLaren (10), Chaparral (6), Wildcat (4) and Phoenix (2).

APPENDIX E:
BRITISH HILLCLIMB CHAMPIONSHIP WINS

	Driver	Car
1977	Alister Douglas-Osborn	Pilbeam MP22-DFV
1990	Martyn Griffiths	Pilbeam MP58-DFR
1991	Martyn Griffiths	Pilbeam MP58-DFR
1992	Roy Lane	Pilbeam MP58-DFL
1993	David Grace	Pilbeam MP58-DFR
1994	David Grace	Pilbeam MP58-DFR
1995	Andy Priaulx	Pilbeam MP58-DFV
1998	David Grace	Gould GR37-DFR
1999	David Grace	Gould GR37-DFR
2000	David Grace	Gould GR37-DFR

In the British Hillclimb Championship the most successful chassis powered by DFV-family engines has been the Pilbeam MP58 (six championship wins) and the most successful driver David Grace (five championship wins).

General

Layout: Four-stroke petrol engine, eight cylinders arranged in two banks of four with 90-degree included angle; 32 valves operated by double overhead camshafts on each cylinder bank
Bore: 85.67mm (3.375in)
Stroke: 64.90mm (2.55in)
Swept volume: 2,993cc (183ci)
Bore/stroke: 1.32:1
Compression ratio: Approximately 11:1

Cylinder block, crankcase and bearings

Block: Asymmetric light alloy casting extending down to crankshaft centreline; wet cast iron cylinder liners pressed into place, located by top flanges and sealed at the base by O-rings; upper face of block has machined recesses for O-ring water seals
Lower crankcase: Separate light alloy lower casting carrying caps for five main bearings and lower chassis mounting points at front corners; lateral and longitudinal tubes integral with lower crankcase casting resist structural loads and carry cooling water across the engine; venting at number 2 and number 4 main bearings
Minimum cylinder spacing: 104.1mm (4.1in)
Cylinder stagger: Left bank 9.5mm (0.375in) ahead of right bank

Cylinder heads

Construction: Light alloy castings with pent-roof combustion chambers, each containing two inlet and two exhaust valves; valve seat and valve guide inserts; heads interchangeable between cylinder banks
Inlet ports: Inclined towards centre of engine on both cylinder banks; ports to each combustion chamber merge into a single inlet tract inside the head
Exhaust ports: Inclined towards outside of engine on both cylinder banks; ports to each combustion chamber merge into a single inlet tract inside the head
Fixings: Ten studs tapped into cylinder block casting and eight bolts retained by nuts under flanges on the block
Spark plug: 10mm Autolite at the cylinder axis

Camshafts, valves and valve gear

Valve operation: Double overhead camshafts per cylinder bank, driven from the crankshaft by a geartrain; direct operation of valves through bucket tappets
Camshaft carriers: Cast light alloy cam carrier above each cylinder head carries guide bores for tappets and the lower half of the five camshaft bearings; cam carrier is reinforced with a longitudinal tube to accept chassis loads carried through front end of cam cover casting and suspension loads at rear end
Camshafts: Chilled iron, eight-lobe camshafts
Camshaft/auxiliary drive: Geartrain driven by crankshaft drives a half-speed shaft in the 'V', which drives camshafts and auxiliaries; upper driveshaft powers fuel injection metering unit, ignition distributor and alternator; toothed belt drive to oil pumps and water pumps
Valve springs: Twin helical, variable-pitch valve springs on each valve

Inlet valve diameter: 34.5mm (1.32in)
Inlet valve angle: 16 degrees to cylinder axis, inclined towards engine centre
Exhaust valve diameter: 29.0mm (1.14in)
Exhaust valve angle: 16 degrees to cylinder axis, inclined away from engine centre

Pistons and connecting rods

Construction: Light alloy with flat crowns, solid skirts and small valve cut-outs
Piston rings: Three: Dykes compression ring, plain second ring and lower oil scraper ring
Connecting rods: Steel forgings split across the big ends at 90 degrees to the rod shank
Big end bearings: Steel-backed lead indium shells
Rod length: 5.23in
Rod/crank throw ratio: 4.1:1

Crankshaft, bearings and clutch

Layout: Single plane, fully counter-balanced
Construction: Steel forging, machined all over and nitrided; crank pins drilled to reduce weight and plugged
Weight: 32lb (14.5kg)
Main bearings: Five, steel-backed with lead indium wear surfaces
Main bearing diameter: 60.3mm
Rod bearing diameter: 49.2mm
Flywheel: Eight-bolt flange at rear of crankshaft with 9.7in flywheel carrying integral starter ring gear
Clutch: Borg and Beck twin-plate clutch with diaphragm spring operation; 7.5in sintered plates

Lubrication system

Layout: Dry sump system
Scavenge pumps: Twin scavenge pumps mounted on the right-hand side, serving front and rear halves of the engine respectively, driven by toothed belt from half-speed auxiliary shaft
Pressure pump: Rotor-type pump on left-hand side of crankcase, driven by toothed belt from half-speed auxiliary shaft

Ignition and Electrical

Electrical system: 12 volt; 9A alternator
Ignition system: Lucas Lutronic transistorised ignition triggered by electromagnetic impulse at approximately 35 degrees before top dead centre
Distributor: Lucas
Spark plugs: 10mm Autolite
Cylinder order: From front: right bank 1-4, left bank 5-8
Firing order: 1-8-3-6-4-5-2-7
Fuel system: Lucas Mk1 mechanical fuel injection; fuel injected downstream into intake ports; variable stroke controlled by throttle opening; mixture adjustable at fuel cam for cold running; electric fuel pump for starting, mechanical pump takes over above 2,000rpm

Cooling

Water pumps: Two centrifugal water pumps, one each side of crankcase, driven by toothed belt from half-speed auxiliary shaft

Dimensions

Length: (front cover to flywheel face) 545mm (21.45in)
Width: 686mm (27in)
Crankshaft centreline to base of sump: 133mm (5.25in)
Weight: (with clutch) approximately 370lb (168kg)

Performance

Maximum power: 408bhp at 9,000rpm
Maximum torque: 270lb ft at 7,000rpm
Maximum BMEP: 223psi
Specific power: 136bhp per litre
Power to weight: 1.14bhp/lb

DFV variants

DFW

2.5-litre conversion of DFV for Tasman series with standard bore but 54mm stroke. Engines built up as DFWs were subsequently converted back to DFV specification. Power output 358bhp at 9,750rpm.

DFX

2.65-litre turbocharged derivative for USAC/CART racing. Retained standard bore, but stroke reduced to 57.30mm (2.256in) for a swept volume of 2,643cc. Power output 720bhp at 11,000rpm (with boost restricted to 48in Hg).

DFL

Long-distance sports car racing derivative. Three phases gradually increasing displacement. First with 90mm (3.543in) bore and standard stroke to increase capacity to 3,298cc. Second with standard bore and 77.7mm (3.06in) stroke for a capacity of 3,583cc Ultimately used 90mm bore and 77.7mm stroke for 3,955cc, in which form the maximum power was approximately 540bhp at 9,250rpm.

DFY

Revised DFV for F1, ultimately with short stroke, redesigned cylinder heads and reduced weight. Ultra-narrow-angle cylinder heads mounted inlets at 10 degrees to cylinder axis, exhausts at 12.5 degrees. Weight down to 292lb, power up to around 540bhp at 11,000rpm by 1984.

DFR

'Atmo' 3.5-litre F1 engine for Tyrrell, AGS and others in 1987. Maximum power initially 595bhp at 11,000rpm.

DFS

Heavily reworked DFX turbo engine using DFR technology. Power output not revealed, but probably about 720bhp.

INDEX